The Basic Book of Sewing

The Basic Book of
Sewing

by Eve Harlow

Octopus Books

Acknowledgements:

Photographers: Alan Meek: pages 2, 11, 22,
47, 50, 59, 70, 74, 75, 79, 83, 87,
111, 114, 118, 122, 123, 126
John Gill: pages 15, 90, 91,
95, 98, 102, 103, 107.
Cover photograph:
John Webb

Dressmaking diagrams on pages 9–60 by
courtesy of McCall's Pattern
Company

Fabrics and haberdashery from John Lewis
Partnership, Oxford Street,
London W1

Accessories and clothes from D. H. Evans Ltd.,
Oxford Street, London W1

First published 1973 by
Octopus Books Limited
59 Grosvenor Street, London W1

ISBN 0 7064 0352 5

© 1973 Octopus Books Limited

Distributed in U.S.A. by
Crescent Books, a division of Crown Publishers Inc
419 Park Avenue South, New York, N.Y.10016

Distributed in Australia by
Rigby Limited
30 North Terrace, Kent Town, Adelaide, South
Australia 5067

Filmset by Photoprint Plates Limited,
Rayleigh, Essex

Produced by Mandarin Publishers Limited
14 Westlands Road, Quarry Bay, Hong Kong

Printed in Hong Kong

Frontispiece:
Pleated skirt (pattern, page 125)

Contents

Introduction

Sewing can be such fun. You have probably heard this said before and wondered if it could possibly be true. Well, it *can* be fun – but much of the enjoyment of sewing as a real hobby comes from the satisfaction of knowing that you are going to turn out something good enough to wear! This confidence depends on knowing the basic techniques of sewing and on knowing how to choose and use paper patterns and fabrics.

The pleasures of sewing

This book is planned to introduce you to sewing. It is not a *complete* course in the craft – that would take several volumes – but all the basic knowhow and techniques you need to be able to make simple garments are explained here. You are shown how to pin out a pattern properly and the right way to cut out is described (usually a most frightening step for a beginner, but once you know how, you will never be afraid).
The following chapters take the beginner dressmaker through all the stages of putting a garment together and all are explained in the simplest possible way. There is even a chapter on those decorative touches which

can add distinction to hand-made things.
If you have never sewn before, it is suggested that you read these chapters very carefully indeed, perhaps reading them twice over before starting your first garment. Once you have got the principles well in your mind, you will be so much more confident and your first project is more likely to be a success. Familiarize yourself with where the different techniques and lessons are in the book so that you can refer back to them quickly if you need to refresh your memory while you are making something.
There are many reasons why women want to learn about dressmaking. Often, of course, it is for economy because it is still possible to make clothes for half the price of those you can buy in the shops – and usually the finish and fabric of one's own handmades is far better!
A love of fashion might start you off too. Many women like to wear up-to-the-moment fashions and the commercial paper pattern companies now produce patterns for the newest styles almost as soon as the fashion shows are over. It is a marvellous feeling to be wearing a fashion that is really new and to know that *your*

particular choice of fabric for that style has made your dress absolutely exclusive!

Being a non-average size and shape might be another reason for taking up dressmaking as a hobby. Anyone who is over six feet tall or under four feet ten inches, excessively thin or more comfortably plump will know how difficult it is to find really well-fitting and flattering clothes. After all, the manufacturers cannot cater for every size and shape.

These are all good reasons for learning to make your own clothes.

Patterns for you to try

When you have read the chapters on techniques carefully, you will be ready to try making some of the clothes in the Pattern Book at the back of the book. The patterns in this section are given as graph patterns but do not be afraid of them – they are very easy to work with once you know how.

Graph patterns are simply full-sized garment patterns scaled down to the size of a page. They are designed in exactly the same way as the paper patterns one buys – the only difference is that the graph pattern is a kind of small master plan from which you draw up your own personal pattern.

The advantage of graph patterns is that one can easily make alterations for size or even for style while one is drawing the pattern out and, if the alterations are actually marked onto the graph itself, the alterations are there to remind you when the pattern is wanted again at a later date.

Instructions are given for drawing up graph patterns. Start with one of the simpler outlines, such as the man's apron or the pinafore dress and in almost no time at all, you'll be quite at ease with graph patterns.

All the designs in the pattern book have been especially chosen for beginners, but more experienced dressmakers will enjoy them too. The clothes are simple and all use the basic sewing techniques; their charm and attractiveness lies in the finish and the choice of fabrics.

Colours and fabrics

Choosing fabrics is one of the most important aspects of home dress making. There is a world of difference between a 'hand-made' look and a 'home-made' look and an unsuitable fabric matched up with an unflattering style is the biggest give-away. The chapter on fabric and style will tell you the secrets of training your eye and developing your fabric colour sense.

Ideas with the patterns

Did you think you were too big for stripes or have you a secret yearning to wear scarlet crepe? Perhaps you can and perhaps a different kind of pattern or fabric colour could change your appearance *and* boost your morale. And perhaps you have never been absolutely sure what your figure type is when you are choosing a paper pattern? The useful figure type charts on pages 16 and 17 will prove an invaluable aid.

Many of the patterns can be adapted to give you an even wider choice of garments. The pretty hostess apron, for instance, could be made full-length with a frill added to the hem and a bib-front added to the waist band. The pinafore dress is so simply cut that it could be cut to hip length for a jerkin to wear over trousers and the long evening dress is so classic in style that it has a variety of possible adaptations. It can be cut short for informal parties, be made up in a summer fabric for a neat day dress or, cut to just below the waist, the design makes a simple shell blouse to wear under a suit.

Fashion is going through a most exciting period when we can wear almost anything we like, at any time and anywhere. Making your own clothes, you will find, is a most satisfying way of expressing your individuality and creativity and knowing how to make them really professionally is one of the secrets of being always well-dressed.

Choosing styles, measuring and altering

Choosing the right style

Although the simple styles given as graph patterns later in this book are intended to start you off on dressmaking, sooner or later you are going to use a commercial paper pattern. Choosing the right style for your figure type is one of the most

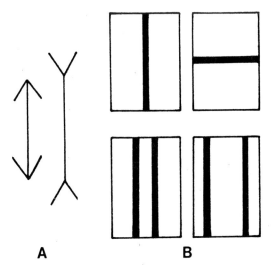

A   **B**

A change in line direction can alter the length of a line or size of an area

important parts of learning to make your own clothes. Too often, a dressmaker chooses a style because she likes it in the catalogue, without really considering whether it will suit her or not and then she is disappointed in the final result. The design of a pattern and the fabric itself can flatter you into looking exactly how you want to look. You can look taller, shorter or slimmer. The right style can add roundness exactly where your figure needs it or can distract the eye away from those areas where you wish you were slimmer. The trick is to fool the eye and the rules are simple. Study the geometric diagrams given here and note how the direction of the arrow heads can make the vertical lines seem longer or shorter (A). Look at the boxed vertical and horizontal lines (B). The dimensions of the boxes are exactly the same in each case but see how the vertical line makes the box appear taller.

How to look taller

The rules of fooling the eye are simple: to create the illusion of looking taller, the eye has to be carried up and down the figure. In garment design, this can be achieved by long pleats, long seams and long sleeves. If the eye is stopped at any point, such as by a wide contrasting colour belt, then the effect becomes shorter. Sheath-shaped dresses, straight front fastenings, Princess lines and long, tight sleeves will all help to give a tall look. Necklines also need to be vertical in effect – V-necklines are good and so are open collars. Round or square necklines stop the eye and so shorten the look of the neck.

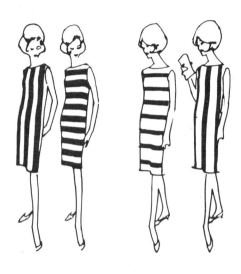

The width of stripes and the spaces between can make a figure look taller or shorter

How to look shorter

To create a wider or more rounded effect on a figure, the design of the garment should encourage the eye to move from side to side or diagonally rather than up and down. In this case, stopping the eye helps the effect and is achieved by designs which have a break at the hipline, either by a seam or by a change in colour, by big patch pockets, and by full sleeves. Jackets and tunics which cut across the hipline help to make the figure look shorter and large collars can shorten the length between shoulder and waist.

Figure faults and solving them

Almost everyone has a figure fault which they would like to correct. By choosing the right style of pattern and, to a certain extent, the right fabric, most figure faults can be camouflaged by dressmaking. A collar line, for instance, which draws attention to a pretty face or a shapely bust is obviously going to mean less attention for over-sized hips! The chart on the following page, worked out by a well-known paper pattern company, gives some useful solutions for common figure faults. Bear them in mind when you are choosing your first commercial paper pattern.

Matching colours to styles

Colours of fabrics can appear to correct figure faults too. Black, as everyone knows, makes one's measurements appear smaller but it also tends to outline the shape. If the outline isn't quite perfect, choose dark grey or brown instead – they are just as slimming but the effect tends to blend you into the background more. This general rule applies to any figure area which is out of proportion to the rest of the body – wearing light or bright contrasts of colour tends to emphasise a fault. Those people with short, plump figures should go for one-colour outfits and choose soft fabrics rather than crisp ones. If prints are worn, clearly-defined patterns should be avoided.

Tall, heavily built women also look

For accuracy, get someone to help with measuring

FIGURE FLAW	SUITABLE SOLUTIONS
Hip Heavy	Create interest at neck and shoulder line. Broaden shoulder Line.
Small Bust	Softly draped bodices, collars, decorative bodice details.
Large Bust	Soft draping, simple necklines, surplice closings, long or ¾ sleeves.
Thick Rib Cage	Boxy jackets, bloused bodices, soft draping and overblouses.
Short-Waisted	Low waisted designs, hip length jackets and overblouses. Smooth, uninterrupted lines.
Long-Waisted	Wide sashes, set-in midriffs, contrasting belts, tunics, peplums, long jackets.
Round shoulders	Place shoulder seam back of its normal position. Use set-in sleeves. Blouse with soft fullness at back. Collar to fill hollow at back. Collared boleros and jackets.
Narrow Shoulders	Set-in sleeves narrowly padded.
Short Neck	Collarless style, V- or U-shaped necklines, standaway collars.
Long Neck	Turtle and mandarin necklines, large collars, high chokers.
Prominent Abdomen	Pleats or shirring at sides of a skirt, creating a straight front panel. Boxy hip length jackets, vertical lines.
Prominent Derrière	Hip length boxy jackets, box pleated flared skirts, shirred waistlines.

better in soft fabrics and should avoid large patterns and shiny surfaced materials.

The tall, thin type of figure can wear bright colours as these tend to add fullness to a shape and colour contrasts should be worn at the waistline or hips – such as belts – to make the figure seem more shapely.

Measuring up

After deciding on the style of garment you're going to make, the next point to aim for is perfect fit. All paper patterns are made to standard measurements and, because there are variations in figure types, to different sizes within the figure types. Even

YOUR PERSONAL MEASUREMENTS CHART

			inches
1	**BUST**	Measure over fullest part of bust and around back	
2	**WAIST**	On natural waistline	
3	**HIPS**	Measure over highest part of buttocks and the thickest part of the thighs	
4	**SHOULDER**	Measure from the base of neck	
5	**ACROSS BACK**	From armhole seam to armhole seam	
6	**BACK LENGTH**	From nape to waist	
7	**CENTRE FRONT**	From base of front neck to waist	
8	**FRONT WIDTH**	From armhole seam to seam, taken between shoulder and bustline	
9	**BUST POINT**	From centre shoulder to highest point of bust	
10	**ARMHOLE**	Over shoulder, around underarm and back to shoulder, taken with arm against body	
11	**SIDE SEAM**	From under armhole to waist	
12	**UNDERARM SLEEVE**	From lowest point of armhole to wrist with arm extended	
13	**OUTSIDE SLEEVE**	From halfway between shoulder and underarm, over bent elbow to wrist	
14	**CENTRE BACK, FULL LENGTH**	From nape, to waist to hem	
15	**SKIRT LENGTH**	From waist line, over hip bone to hem	
16	**DEPTH OF CRUTCH**	(for trousers) From centre front waistline, through crutch to centre back waist	
17	**INSIDE LEG**	With legs apart, measure from inside crutch to ankle bone	

though you might have exactly the same bust, waist and hips measurement as your friend, this doesn't mean that your figure shape is the same; the waist and bust positions may be entirely different. On page 16, you will find charts, specially prepared by one of the leading commercial paper pattern companies to help the home dressmaker choose the correct paper pattern for her size and shape.

By checking your own measurements against those on the charts, you will be able to select the pattern with the best possible fit for you.

The graph patterns in this book are given in size 12 – that is, bust 34 inches, waist 25–26 inches and hips 36 inches. You will be shown how to adapt the graphs to fit you own measurements. First of all however, you need to know exactly what your measurements are. Enlist the help of a friend or your husband to help you take them accurately.

Measuring children

One rarely needs to make children's clothes as closely fitting as adults' so fewer measurements are needed. The length of back, from neck to waist, back waist to hem, shoulder to wrist, chest, waist, inside leg and round the neck will suffice. One further measurement is essential if the child tends to have a pot belly – and most do when small – and that is the measurement from the base of the front neck to the hem, taken over the stomach.

Take measurements over a close-fitting sweater or slip. Pin a length of tape around the waist first – this

helps to achieve exact bodice length measurements.

Adapting paper patterns to fit

Some people's measurements vary slightly from the average and it may be necessary to alter paper patterns to achieve an even better fit. Alterations are made on the paper pattern itself and commercial paper patterns are usually marked with lines where alterations to depth and width can be made.

To alter a pattern piece, cut through the paper with scissors and spread the pieces the amount to be altered. Tape a strip of tissue paper between the spread pieces and redraw any lines or markings to keep the original shape of the pattern.

To shorten pattern pieces, crease the paper across the guide lines given, pleating up the amount to be taken out. Pin and then redraw the lines to retain the original shape of the pattern.

The Pattern Book

The graph patterns in the Pattern Book are given only in size 12, to make it easier for beginners to draft patterns. However, it is a simple matter to alter patterns to sizes 10, 14 and in some cases to size 16 by adding to and subtracting from the overall width of the pattern.

Altering skirts

Draw the pattern pieces out on squared paper as instructed and then

Children's dresses (patterns, pages 100 and 104)

Commercial paper patterns are made not only to figure measurements but also to fit figure types. Check your measurements with the charts here to determine your figure type when choosing paper patterns.

MISSES'

Misses' patterns are designed for a well proportioned, and developed figure; about 5'5" to 5'6" without shoes.

Size	6	8	10	12	14	16	18	20
Bust	30½	31½	32½	34	36	38	40	42
Waist	23	24	25	26½	28	30	32	34
Hip	32½	33½	34½	36	38	40	42	44
Back Waist Length	15½	15¾	16	16¼	16½	16¾	17	17¼

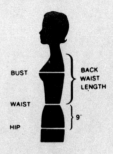

WOMEN'S

Women's patterns are designed for the larger, more fully mature figure; about 5'5" to 5'6" without shoes.

Size	38	40	42	44	46	48	50
Bust	42	44	46	48	50	52	54
Waist	35	37	39	41½	44	46½	49
Hip	44	46	48	50	52	54	56
Back Waist Length	17¼	17⅜	17½	17⅝	17¾	17⅞	18

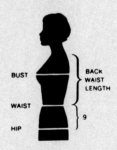

HALF-SIZE

Half-size patterns are for a fully developed figure with a short backwaist length. Waist and hip are larger in proportion to bust than other figure types: about 5'2" to 5'3" without shoes.

Size	10½	12½	14½	16½	18½	20½	22½	24½
Bust	33	35	37	39	41	43	45	47
Waist	27	29	31	33	35	37½	40	42½
Hip	35	37	39	41	43	45½	48	50½
Back Waist Length	15	15¼	15½	15¾	15⅞	16	16⅛	16¼

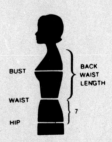

JUNIOR PETITE

Junior Petite patterns are designed for a well proportioned petite figure, about 5' to 5'1" without shoes.

Size	3jp	5jp	7jp	9jp	11jp	13jp
Bust	30½	31	32	33	34	35
Waist	22½	23	24	25	26	27
Hip	31½	32	33	34	35	36
Back Waist Length	14	14¼	14½	14¾	15	15¼

JUNIOR

Junior patterns are designed for a well proportioned shorter waisted figure, about 5'4" to 5'5" without shoes.

Size	5	7	9	11	13	15
Bust	30	31	32	33½	35	37
Waist	22½	23	24	25	27	29
Hip	32	33	34	35½	37	39
Back Waist Length	15	15¼	15½	15¾	16	16¼

YOUNG JUNIOR/TEEN

This new size range is designed for the developing pre-teen and teen figures; about 5'1" to 5'3" without shoes.

Size	5/6	7/8	9/10	11/12	13/14	15/16
Bust	28	29	30½	32	33½	35
Waist	22	23	24	25	26	27
Hip	31	32	33½	35	36½	38
Back Waist Length	13½	14	14½	15	15⅜	15¾

GIRLS'

Girls' patterns are designed for the girl who has not yet begun to mature. See chart below for approximate heights without shoes.

Size	7	8	10	12	14
Breast	26	27	28½	30	32
Waist	23	23½	24½	25½	26½
Hip	27	28	30	32	34
Back Waist Length	11½	12	12¾	13½	14¼
Approx. Heights	50"	52"	56"	58½"	61"

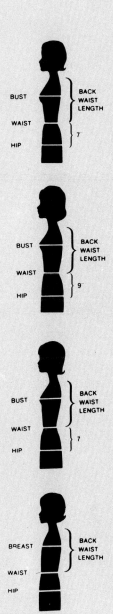

Reproduced by permission of McCalls Pattern Company Limited.

redraw the side seams to the new measurements. To decrease a hipline one size (2 inches), divide the amount by four and take an equal amount off each side seam allowance ($\frac{1}{2}$ inch), front and back pieces. Adjust the

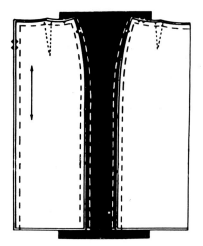

Method for increasing the hipline of a skirt pattern

waist measurement to size and taper the line off to the hem.

To increase the hip measurements by one size (2 inches), divide the total amount to be added by four and add equally to the seam allowances, front and back pieces.

Altering bodices

It is trickier to alter the size of bodice pieces by this method because alterations to the side seams affect the size of the armholes and this in

turn means altering the crown of the sleeve – a difficult exercise for a beginner.

A simpler method for achieving a straightforward increase or decrease in width is to cut the pattern from just below the shoulder line to the waist on both sides of the bodice and then across the bodice. Cut and spread the pieces for the increase in size required. Pleat and pin for a decrease in size.

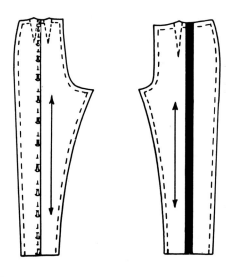

Trouser patterns are altered by slashing the length of the pattern piece

Many of the patterns in the Pattern Book can be adapted in this way and where this is possible, the patterns are marked with a dotted line to show the best place to cut and spread or pleat.

Fabrics and linings

All about fabrics

The next important subject in dressmaking is the fabric. There are some important things to know about the structure of fabric and some words and phrases which you need to be familiar with because they keep occurring in dressmaking instructions.

Grain and bias

All woven fabrics, whether made of natural fibres such as cotton, wool or linen or man-made fibre, are composed of two sets of threads that run at right angles to each other. The lengthwise threads (the warp), are called the *lengthwise grain* and the selvedge is the lengthwise finished edge on each side of the fabric.
The crosswise threads are called *the weft* and are referred to as the *crosswise grain*.
Bias refers to the diagonal of the fabric and *true bias* is the term used for the edge formed when the fabric is folded diagonally so that the crosswise threads run in the same direction as the lengthwise threads. Pattern pieces are usually marked with a heavy line with an arrowhead at each end to indicate that the pattern is to be placed to the lengthwise grain of the fabric. Some pieces – facings, collars and cuffs for instance – might be indicated to be cut on the bias to take advantage of the stretch in the fabric.

Napped or pile fabrics

Sometimes you will see that commercial pattern fabric requirements give a different quantity for fabrics 'with nap' and 'without nap'.
'With nap', in dressmaking, means a fabric with a pile (or nap), such as velvet, or with shading or with a one way design.
'Without nap' of course, means a fabric without a pile or nap and with a design which can be used any way round.

Choosing fabrics

Commercial paper patterns usually give the home dressmaker a good selection of fabrics to choose from when making up their designs. It is wiser to stick to their choice of fabrics unless you are very experienced because the weight and weave of the material are important if perfect fit and hang are to be achieved.
If the design is unsuitable for a

oneway or definite pattern, such as stripes, the fabric suggestions will tell you so.

A beginner might be tempted to use a very cheap fabric for her first attempt at dressmaking. It is understandable that she does not want to risk waste but it is unwise to do this. Cheap fabrics hardly ever make up into good-looking garments, but if you buy the best fabric you can afford, your time and effort in dressmaking are unlikely to be wasted. Good fabrics are often much easier to work with.

Fibres and finishes

Over the past twenty years, great advances have been made by fibre manufacturers, spinners, weavers and knitters in producing easy-care fabrics of every kind and in achieving special finishes.

It is important to be able to recognise a man-made fibre and to know its qualities. It is perhaps even more important to be able to recognise a special finish on a fabric and to know whether it is easy to handle in dressmaking and whether it should be washed or dry-cleaned.

Ask the shop assistant for all the information she can give you about a fabric before you buy it; will it wash, does it need ironing, will it dry-clean? There is not much point in making up an every-day dress in a white linen-type rayon if it is going to spend most of the time at the dry-cleaners!

Always test a fabric for crease-resisting qualities before deciding upon it. Crush a corner in your hand – if the creases stay – do not buy it!

Problem fabrics

Although most fabrics are very easy to handle and present no problems to the home dressmaker, there are a few fabrics which require a little expertise in both cutting out and stitching. Beginners are advised to choose firm cotton and woollen fabrics to start with and then they'll be ready to handle other fabrics when they have become more experienced. Knitted fabrics or jersey fabrics for instance are sometimes supplied in tubular form and can be tricky to handle. They are inclined to stretch out of shape as soon as the pieces are cut out and require immediate stay-stitching all round each garment piece.

Fabric quantities

Commercial paper patterns give the quantity of fabric needed in a variety of widths. This is because some weaves and knits are made narrower or wider than is usual. Do not be tempted to economize on the quantity of fabric recommended. The fabric layouts are worked out very carefully for the most economical use of the material and if you should find yourself with a good-sized piece of fabric left over, you can always make a matching cap or beret with it.

Unwrap and shake out your fabric as soon as you get it home or the folds may set into creases which are difficult to remove.

If there are creases in the fabric, press them out before pinning out the paper pattern, taking care to press under a dry cloth.

Linings, underlinings, interlinings and interfacings

All of these terms refer to dressmaking techniques for shaping garments and it is as well to know exactly what they all mean before you begin dressmaking. Each one uses different types of material; some will prevent loosely woven fabrics from sagging, others will give greater crease-resistance and extra firmness to pockets and necklines, while others will enable a detail, like a dramatic collar, to be become firm and stand away from the garment.

Linings

The back of the paper pattern envelope will tell you whether your garment requires lining. Linings are made up separately from the garment and inside out, being attached to the garment from a main seam, such as a shoulder seam. Linings shape a garment, improve its wearability and help to make the inside of a dress or suit look more attractive and well finished.

Underlinings

An underlining has a similar use to a lining but is never used where the fabric is to be draped. It provides backing for a section or sections of a garment where extra body is required.

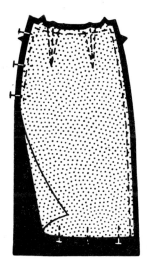

Underlinings are made up with the fabric

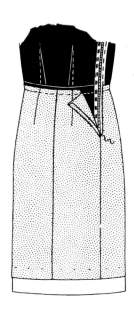

Linings are constructed separately

The underlining is cut out as soon as the garment piece has been cut out and the two pieces are made up together as one. All lining fabrics should be chosen to match the top fabric in both colour and quality. The lining, after all, takes a lot of the wear!

Interlining

This means a fluffy fabric lining, used in tailoring where both shaping and extra warmth are required. Interlining is used between the lining and the fabric, is sometimes made up

separately and is catch-stitched to the garment before the lining is stitched in.

Interfacing

Interfacing is an extra layer of fabric between the facing and the garment itself and its purpose is to give

Interfacing is placed between facing and outer fabric

firmness to one part of the garment and to give a clean edge. It is used to reinforce such areas as a front fastening where there are buttons and buttonholes or between layers of top fabric for collars and cuffs.

Interfacing fabrics must be carefully chosen because it is important that they should strengthen without changing the character of the top fabric.

As a general rule, choose a fabric such as fine lawn or cotton for interfacing light-weight wools and for heavier knits, such as those made of synthetic fibres, choose a non-woven interfacing in a weight to match the top fabric. Cotton organdie is ideal for interfacing fine fabrics or, if the fabric isn't patterned, an extra layer of the actual top fabric works very well.

The non-woven interfacings such as Vilene are economical to use because they haven't a grain and they are washable, but they have one disadvantage in that they have no stretch and so will not make softly moulded collars and cuffs. One type, made from Terylene ('bias facing') has a little more stretch to it and can be used fairly successfully for collars and cuffs.

A beautiful choice of fabrics for the home sewer

Tools and equipment

Dressmaking, like every other craft, is so much easier if you have the right tools for the job. A sewing machine is the main piece of equipment needed and a tremendous advantage to the home dressmaker, helping her to achieve a professional finish. However, lovely clothes *can* be made without a sewing machine, so do not be discouraged if you do not have one. Machines with a swing needle are very efficient, enabling jersey and knitted fabrics to be sewn with ease, but straight stitch machines can cope with most fabrics if the tension, stitch length and thread are carefully chosen. Good machine sewing is the perfect union of thread and fabric, based on the correct thread, the proper needle size, the right tension and the appropriate number of stitches to the inch. Study the manufacturer's instruction book carefully – it pays to understand your sewing machine.

Stocking a work basket

Workbaskets are hardly ever large enough to take all the odds and ends a dressmaker needs but if cotton reels and lengths of elastic, tape and ribbons can be kept separately, it does help to keep things tidy. Store these items in glass jars where you can see what you want at a glance or ask a handyman to make you a little cabinet of drawers. Buttons, hooks and eyes and press studs can be kept in the drawers too.

Keep an eye on haberdashery and notion counters for dressmakers' aids. Lots of clever items can be found to include in your workbasket. Apart from the contents of your workbasket, you will need certain tools. Those listed here are not essential for beginners but they do make the job easier and more fun and are worth considering.

For measuring and pattern making

Ruler. You will need a long flexible ruler, for pattern making, preferably 36 inches long but a 12-inch one will do. A flexible *plastic rule* which bends easily is useful for drawing curves, but not essential.

Tape measure. Choose one made of glass fibre and with metal ends because this type does not stretch. If possible, have one that is marked with both inches and centimeters.

Squared paper. Squared paper can be obtained from stationery shops and from the dressmaking department of some large stores. It comes in sheets measuring 30 inches by 20 inches and is marked into 1 inch, $\frac{1}{2}$ inch and $\frac{1}{4}$ inch squares. It is used for drafting graph patterns and two or three sheets are required for a dress or suit. Sheets are joined together with Sellotape. Brown paper can be used for drafting patterns if squared paper is not easily available but the inch squares have to be drawn out on it very accurately.

Tracing paper. After the graph pattern has been drawn up onto the squared paper, thus making a master pattern, the paper pattern itself is traced off, using tracing paper. This gives you a more flexible pattern and one which is easier to pin – and you can keep the master pattern intact for using again.

For cutting

A pair of scissors should be kept especially for cutting paper. Tie a piece of coloured thread to the handles to keep them separate.

Dressmaking shears. These have long cutting blades and bent handles. They are more accurate in use than ordinary scissors as they lift the fabric less.

Pinking shears. These have notched blades and are used to trim seams on garments made of firmly woven fabrics to prevent fraying.

A small pair of scissors with sharp points should also be included in basic equipment. These are useful for jobs like cutting buttonholes and snipping into seams.

For marking

Tailor's chalk. This comes in white and in colours, in flat cakes or in pencil form. It is used for making pattern markings on smooth fabrics. It is particularly useful for marking alterations on the wrong side of the garment during fitting.

Dressmaker's carbon paper. This is available in sheets and in white, orange or black. To use it, a sheet is placed face downwards on the fabric under the paper pattern and another sheet face upwards under the bottom layer of fabric. The pattern markings are then traced through the paper either by using a *tracing wheel* or with a blunt pencil and ruler.

It is important to work on a flat, hard surface when using dressmaker's carbon paper or there may be distortion in reproduction.

For sewing

Needles. There are several different kinds of needles but for hand sewing a 'sharps' No. 7 is the best. 'Betweens', which are shorter, are used for fine sewing and size No. 8 is ideal; 'straws' are good for tacking jobs.

Sewing machine needles should be selected for thread and fabric following the guide given in the manufacturer's instruction book.

Threads. Pure silk is the best thread for sewing natural fabric but it is expensive and becoming difficult to obtain. Mercerized cotton, available in a wide range of colours, can be used instead.

Modern sewing machines stitch better with a fine gauge thread and Coats' Drima, available in slim spools and in a wide range of colours is ideal for synthetic fabrics and natural fibre fabrics alike. Drima is, however, very strong and should not be used for basting.

Basting thread is available on large-sized reels and machine embroidery thread, No. 30, is good for machine-made buttonholes and for zig-zag seam neatening.

Silk buttonhole twist is used for handworked buttonholes.

Button thread is used for sewing buttons on to heavier garments.

Pins. Choose dressmaker's pins and have a lot of them. Glass-headed dressmaker's pins are very sharp and slightly longer and look very pretty in use. They are easier to pick up too! **A magnet** is a great help for picking up loose pins and needles and for a quick tidy-up after a dressmaking session.

A quick **unpicking tool** is an invaluable aid for ripping seams and for lifting out tacking threads.

Dressmaker's dummy

A dressmaker's dummy or dress stand is by no means essential to dressmaking but it can be useful for fitting if you have nobody to help at this stage. It can also be a great help when putting in linings or placing pockets. Choose one which stands very firmly on its base; some types look very smart and efficient but simply have not the weight to take a garment without falling over. Try to select one with a fabric surface into which you can stick pins.

Press as you go

The golden rule of dressmaking, as any professional will tell you, is to press every seam as it is completed. Get into the habit of pressing at every single stage and you stand a good chance of having a garment which looks really professional.

Always press on the wrong side of the fabric and use a slightly dampened cloth. Always leave the fabric on the ironing board for a minute or two to allow the steam to cool out of it before going on.

The technique of pressing. Pressing is a quite different technique from ironing. Ironing is a smoothing movement, pressing is lifting the iron and putting it down again firmly,

using the other hand to control the fabric.

Equipment for pressing

Ironing board. An ordinary ironing board will do and if possible, have a sleeve board as well that will stand on a table, for pressing small areas. The table will support the weight of the garment.

Seam roll. Make one from a 12-inch length of wood, such as a broom handle, and pad it with flannelette sheeting. Use this under seams as a pressing aid.

Tailor's ham. This is useful for pressing darts and is made with two oval pieces of cotton sheeting, about 15 inches by 10. The oval should have a narrow end, rather like the shape of an egg. Stitch the two pieces together and stuff with sawdust if possible or with scraps of fabric; the ham must be really firmly packed. The surface should be completely smooth and it may be necessary to make one or two small darts in the fabric to achieve this.

Pressing mitt. This can be purchased from haberdashery shops; it is quite useful for pressing rounded areas of garments but is not essential equipment.

Pressing cloth. Butter muslin makes the best pressing cloth. Lay it on the fabric before applying the iron, so that you press through it.

Point presser. This is a useful piece of equipment for pushing out collar points or the corners of pocket flaps. Wind a strip of soft fabric round the end of a large-sized knitting needle so that it is not too sharp.

Tools and equipment (Photograph by J & P Coats Ltd)

26

Techniques and stitches

Dressmaking is a skill and to become really expert requires an extensive knowledge of the techniques involved and a great deal of practise. However, even a beginner can learn to make simply designed clothes if she has a good working knowledge of the basic sewing techniques.

The techniques on the following pages are planned to take a beginner-dressmaker through the various stages of putting a garment together, from pinning out the pattern on the fabric to making a perfect hem. You might wish to practise some of the more tricky techniques, such as bound buttonholes, on scraps of fabric first before attempting them on a garment.

Have all your equipment to hand before you start a dressmaking project. Most important of all, put the ironing board up and have the iron and pressing materials ready for work. A good dressmaker keeps her ironing board up all the time her sewing machine is in use. Pressing at every stage is absolutely essential for a good finish to a garment.

Laying out the pattern

Ideally, a large table should be used for cutting out but if this is not possible, use the floor, preferably an area without carpet.

Follow the fabric layout given with your paper pattern and fold the fabric as shown. Lay out the entire paper pattern on the fabric before attempting to cut out a single piece and take careful note of those pieces which are to be placed along the fold of the fabric. Place each piece of pattern so that the grain line (the heavy line with an arrow head at each end), follows the lengthwise grain or bias of the fabric.

Some pattern pieces will say 'cut 2' which you will do automatically as you cut from the folded double thickness of fabric. Where the pieces indicate that you are to 'cut 1', cut from a single thickness.

Pinning out

Do not cut out anything until you are absolutely sure that every piece of pattern is placed on the fabric correctly. First, place pins at each end of, and in the centre of, the grain lines. Next, pin pieces which are placed along the fold of the fabric. Place pins within the seam allowance at right angles to the cut edges, points towards the edge, but not so that the shears will touch the points.

Space pins about 6 inches apart and take up only a few threads of fabric so that the fabric lies as flat as possible.

Cutting out

Now comes the stage that every beginner dreads – actually cutting into the fabric. You have nothing to fear if you have pinned out every piece correctly, so check once more. A danger is where patterns show sleeves to be cut separately from single thicknesses of fabric, for economy. In these instances, you will see that on the fabric layout one sleeve is shaded to indicate that the pattern is placed printed side down for the second sleeve. If you miss this point, you will finish up with two sleeves for the right armhole and none for the left and you will have wasted your fabric.

Use bent-handled dressmaker's shears for cutting out because they lift the fabric less and give more accurate cutting out. Use long, steady cuts and if you can learn to cut without completely closing the blades you will get an even edge rather than a ragged one. Cut right on the cutting line and cut outwards round notches rather than inwards. Snip into selvedges if they show signs of pulling.

After cutting out all the pieces, leave the paper patterns pinned to the fabric ready for marking. Cut the remaining fabric up and keep the largest pieces for bias strips, covering buttons, making belts or, if there is enough, making caps and berets.

Marking

There are several methods of transferring the construction markings from the paper pattern to the fabric but the most reliable method is tailor's tacking. It might not seem the quickest method and many authorities recommend other ways as being easier. Tailor's tacks can, however, be made quite quickly, they can be used on any kind of fabric and they are a very accurate method of marking.

Tailor's tacks

Using doubled thread in a contrasting colour to that of the fabric, take a small stitch, at the point to be marked, through both fabric and pattern paper, leaving an inch of thread end. Take a second stitch in the same place leaving a small loop. The two layers of fabric are pulled gently apart and the threads cut between the layers leaving a tuft marking the position of the symbol. Markings which are close together can be marked without cutting the thread providing that enough thread is left between each tailor's tack.

Basting

Basting marks (see p. 31) are used along grain lines in those instances where it is important to keep to the grain of a fabric, such as garments cut on the cross; they can also be used for marking buttonholes and placing pleats and trimmings.

Tracing wheel and carbon

This method of marking works on most fabrics but it cannot be used on sheer fabrics where the marks would show through the completed garment, or on heavily napped fabrics where the marks would not show at all. Use

only dressmaker's carbon paper and test the colour first on a scrap of the fabric to make sure that the marks show clearly. Place the carbon paper under the paper pattern, face down on the fabric and run the wheel along the lines to be marked, using the straight edge of a ruler as a guide. Mark circular symbols with two short crossed lines.

Tailor's chalk and pins

A tailor's chalk pencil is used as it can be sharpened to a good point. Place pins through the fabric and paper pattern at the points to be marked. Remove the paper pattern carefully and mark the position of the pins with tailor's chalk.

Stay-stitching

Patterns sometimes indicate that a row of stay-stitching be worked on a single thickness of fabric close to the seamline – necklines and shoulder seams are often stitched in this way. Stay-stitching helps to prevent edges stretching before the pieces are sewn together and on garments made of jersey fabrics this is often essential. A matching thread is used in the machine and a setting of 12 stitches to the inch. Stay-stitching is worked $\frac{1}{8}$ inch from the seamline ($\frac{1}{2}$ inch from the edge on $\frac{5}{8}$ inch seams). If the fabric is of a type that slips when being machined, baste tissue paper to it before stay-stitching.

Once the construction marks have been transferred from the pattern to

the fabric, the paper pattern can be unpinned. Cut any interfacings at this stage.

Basting

Basting or, as it is sometimes called, tacking, is used to hold two pieces of fabric together temporarily for fitting and for sewing. Basting is best done by hand and in a contrasting thread. There are four types of basting stitches:

Even basting. Even basting is used on seams where there is likely to be some strain. To work: Stitches should be made about $\frac{1}{4}$ inch long on both sides of the fabric.

Uneven basting. A $\frac{1}{2}$ inch stitch is made on the upper side of the fabric and about $\frac{1}{8}$ inch on the underside. Uneven basting is used for marking or as a guideline for stitching.

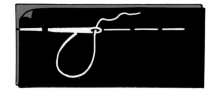

Diagonal basting. This is a useful stitch for keeping several layers of fabric together. To work: Sew at right angles to the fabric edge, a diagonal stitch appearing on the upper side of the fabric and a short vertical one on the wrong side.

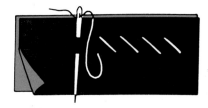

Slip basting. Slip basting is most useful where stripes or plaids need to be matched. To work: turn under the seam allowance on one side and press flat. Place this over the other section, right side up, and match the seam line. Take a small stitch on the seam line of the undersection, bring the needle through the seamline of the top section. Stitches should be kept to about ¼ inch in length and none should show on the right side of the fabric.

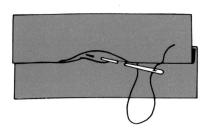

Stitches in dressmaking

Although most dressmaking sewing is done on a sewing machine, there are occasions when hand sewing is necessary, such as putting in zips and finishing hems. The diagrams given are for right-handed people, but if you are left-handed you can convert them to your way of working simply by holding a small hand mirror against the page. All permanent hand sewing should be started and ended with a

back stitch (see below). Never use a knot.

Running stitch. This is the simplest of all hand sewing stitches and is used for gathering, for tucking and for mending jobs. To work, pass the needle in and out through the fabric, taking four or more stitches at a time before pulling the thread through. The stitches should be very small and neat.

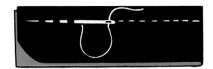

Back stitch. Properly done, back stitching resembles machine stitching on the right side but the stitches overlap on the wrong side. All hand sewing stitches should begin and end with one or two back stitches; back stitching is also used where particularly strong hand sewing is required.

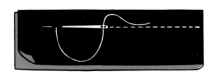

To work, bring the needle through from the wrong side of the fabric. Take a stitch *back* ⅛ inch from where the needle came through and then bring the needle through ⅛ inch in front. Continue in the same way.

Pick stitch. This is worked in a similar way to back stitch except that the needle picks up only two or three threads going back and comes out

32

$\frac{1}{4}$ inch ahead. Pick stitch is used for such jobs as inserting a zip fastener by hand.

Slip stitch. Slip stitch is useful where an invisible finish is needed. To work, pick up one thread of the under section and then take $\frac{1}{8}$ inch stitch through the fold of the top fabric. Pick up the next stitch immediately below in the undersection.

Hemming stitch. Once a much loved stitch in delicate hand sewing, hemming stitch is now used for such jobs as applying the facing to the backs of buttonholes. To work, pick up one thread of the garment and then pass the needle through the folded edge of the hem.

Invisible stitch. This is sometimes called French stitch, perhaps because it is used extensively in tailoring and haute couture clothes. It is used for attaching facings and interfacings and for finishing hems.

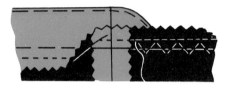

To work, turn the hem or facing back on the garment. Working from right to left pick up a thread of the garment and then pick up a thread from *under* the hem or facing above, working diagonally. The stitches should fall between the two layers of fabric.

Seams and darts

Stitch a neat seam

Unless otherwise marked, all the seam allowances both in commercial paper patterns and graph patterns are $\frac{5}{8}$ inch. The method of sewing used for a seam is determined both by the fabric and by the position of the seam on the garment.

Plain seam. This seam is the most commonly used for joining sections of a garment together. The machine stitch is set to the number of stitches to an inch recommended by the manufacturer for that particular fabric. Pin the two pieces of fabric together and baste along the seam

Machining a plain seam over pin basting

line. Machine stitch on the seam line, following the direction given in the pattern. Finish off at both ends either by tying a double knot in the two threads, by making a double back stitch or, if the machine has one,

by operating a forward and reverse motion.

Zigzag seams. Zigzag seams can only be worked on sewing machines with a swing needle but they are particularly good for seams on knitted fabrics where some 'give' is required. A narrow, closely spaced zigzag stitch should be used. Zigzag stitching can also be used effectively on seams of garments made of sheer fabrics. The fabric is placed right sides facing, with a fine cord placed along the stitching line. Narrow zigzag stitches are worked along the seam line, over the cord. The seam is then trimmed back close to the stitching and the garment turned to the right side and pressed.

French seam. This is a beautiful seam for sheer fabrics or for fine

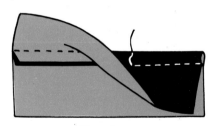

French seam

Stitching a seam (Photograph by Bernina Sewing Machines)

fabrics which are likely to fray. Pin the fabric wrong sides facing and stitch $\frac{3}{8}$ inch from the edge. Press the seam open. Turn the garment to the other side and press flat along the seam line. Stitch $\frac{1}{4}$ inch from the folded edge, thus encasing the raw edges.

Flat fell seam. This seam is used mostly on pyjamas, shirts and children's trousers, sometimes on adults' trousers and jeans. Make a plain seam first with wrong sides of fabric facing. Press the seam open.

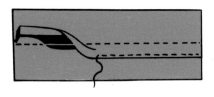

Flat-fell seam

Trim one seam allowance to $\frac{1}{8}$ inch. Turn under the raw edge of the other seam allowance. Press it down over the trimmed edge and top-stitch down to the garment, close to the folded edge.

Useful hints on seams

Grading. Sometimes pattern instructions will suggest 'grading' a seam to reduce bulk. This is usually done where there are more than two layers of fabric, such as an interfaced collar. Grading means cutting the seam allowance to different widths to reduce the thickness of a seam. The seam allowance nearest to the outside fabric is trimmed least while the

interfacing fabric is trimmed as close to the stitching line as possible.

Grading seams

Clipping curves. Pattern instructions will tell you to clip curved seams such as those in necklines. This is to make the curve lie flat. Use a sharply pointed pair of scissors and, for an inward curve (see diagram a) clip into the seam

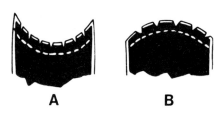

| A | B |

Clipping inward and outward curves

allowance towards the stitching line, stopping about $\frac{1}{8}$ inch from it. Clip at about $\frac{1}{2}$-inch intervals, closer if the curve is pronounced. On an outward curve (see diagram b), cut notches in the fabric to the line of stitching.

Seam finishes

Most fabrics fray to some degree

during wear and the raw edges of seams need to be finished off neatly. There are several methods of doing this.

Pinked edge. Pinked edges, cut with pinking shears, should only be used on fabrics which will not fray; it is not recommended as a method for seam finishing in good dressmaking.

Zigzag finish. Fabrics which are inclined to fray can be finished off with zigzag machine stitching. Press the seam open and machine stitch

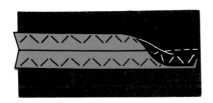

Zigzagged edge

with a medium zigzag close to the raw edge. It is inadvisable to finish underarm seams with zigzag stitching, as it is inclined to be uncomfortable in wear.

Double stitched seam. This is a sturdy finish for seams of garments which are going to be frequently in

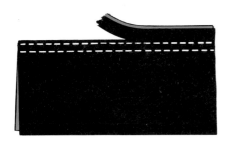

Double-stitched seam

the wash. Stitch a second row about $\frac{1}{4}$ inch away from the original seam line. Trim the fabric away close to the second line of stitching.

Overcasting. Fabrics which fray excessively can have seams overcast by hand. Press the seam open and work a row of machine stitching $\frac{1}{8}$ inch from the raw edges. Working

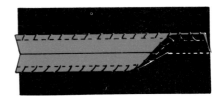

Overcast edge

from left to right, work overcasting over the cut edge and through the machine stitching.

Turned and stitched edges. This is the neatest finish of all and looks very good on the inside of a finished garment. Press the seam open and

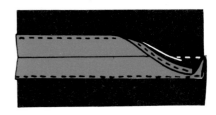

Turned and stitched edge

make a row of machine stitching $\frac{1}{8}$ inch from the raw edges. Turn under a hem along the stitched line and stitch again, close to the folded edge.

Bound edges. This is the most suitable seam finish for loosely woven fabrics. Encase each raw edge with commercial bias binding.

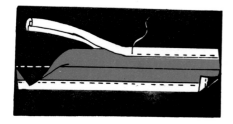

Bound edge

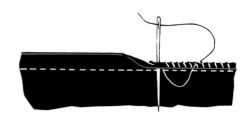

Rolled edge

Rolled edges. This is a pretty finish for sheer fabrics, and is especially suitable for lingerie. Press the seam flat and trim back to $\frac{3}{8}$ inch. Using the thumb and forefinger, roll the seam allowance to the stitching line and sew over the rolled edge close to the stitching line.

Tools and fabric for sewing (Photograph by the International Wool Secretariat)

Making perfect darts

Darts, as you will see from paper patterns, are used for shaping pieces of fabric to the curves of the body. They are usually used under the armhole, running from the side seams for bust shaping, from the shoulder seams and from the waistline, shaping both the waistline and the upper hip area.

Darts are marked with lines and a series of dots on commercial paper patterns and in outline on graph patterns.

Simple darts. Whether the dart to be sewn is a simple triangular dart or a curved dart, the sewing technique is the same.

Fold the dart along the centre, right sides of fabric facing. Pin and then baste firmly (see page 31). Stitch from the widest end towards the point, with the last three stitches on the fold. Secure the ends with forward and reverse machine stitching or tie off the ends tightly. It is *important* to make the last stitches on the fold, to achieve a smooth flow into the fabric and not make an ugly point. Press the dart flat and then press it towards one side. Darts in heavy fabrics can be slashed to within $\frac{1}{2}$ inch of the point after stitching. Press open and oversew the raw edges to prevent fraying.

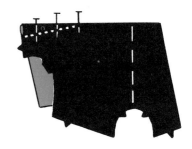

Three stages of making a dart

Bias binding

Necklines and armholes can be given a quick finish with a bound edging made of bias-cut self fabric. Commercially produced cotton bias bindings, available in different widths and colours, are used for finishing off curved seams and make very pretty trims for collar and cuff edgings and for children's clothes.

Cutting bias binding

Bias binding is cut on the true bias of the fabric. To find the true bias, fold the fabric diagonally so that the crosswise grain is parallel to the lengthwise grain. The folded edge is the true bias. Cut along the fold and measure the width of bias binding required from the cut edge. Cut strips diagonally as required.

Joining strips. Place two strips of binding together, right sides facing and at right angles to each other,

Applying binding. Bias binding is cut to twice the width of the finished binding plus seam allowances. Thus, if the finished bound edge is to show $\frac{1}{2}$ inch of binding, cut twice this plus two seam allowances – $2\frac{1}{4}$ inches.

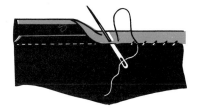

Applying bias binding

Mark the centre of the binding along the length with basting stitches (see page 31). Pin the binding to the garment, right sides facing, so that the marked centre will lie on the raw edge of the garment when the binding is folded over. Baste and then stitch the binding to the garment along the seam line. Turn the binding

Cutting and joining a bias strip

with corners overlapping so that the raw edges will line up with each other after joining. Stitch, then press open the seam and trim away the points that extend over the edges. Always stretch bias binding slightly before using it.

over the raw edge of the garment, turn under the binding seam allowance and hem by hand to the stitching line.

Binding can also be worked from the wrong side of the garment first and then top-stitched on the right side.

Facings

In a well-made garment, every raw edge has to be finished off neatly and facings are one of the techniques used for finishing. Facings are used for the inside fronts of blouses and jackets and for finishing off necklines and armholes. Sometimes, jacket front facings are cut in one with the section of garment and if a heavy fabric is being used the facing is simply folded back and hemmed down on the inside. In some cases however, the pattern instructions may indicate that an *interfacing* is to be cut from part of the facing pattern and used between the top fabric and the facing for greater firmness.

Neckline facings are cut separately from the garment section and are sometimes interfaced. Most paper patterns will instruct that the interfacing should be cut from the facing pattern piece, then machine stitched to the facing along the seam line. In the days before non-woven interfacing fabrics, interfacing was cut to within the seam line and attached to the facing with catch-stitches. This meant that the edges of interfaced pieces were less bulky and cleaner in line. Nowadays, all pattern instructions give the method illustrated here.

Applying facings

Pin and baste the facing to the garment edge, right sides together. Match notches carefully. Stitch the facing down, sewing on the seam line. Grade the seam and clip the curve (see page 36). Press the seam towards the facing. Understitch the facing (see diagram b) to prevent it from rolling to the outside. Turn facing to inside. Neck facings are catch-stitched to the shoulder seams. **Armhole facings** are worked in exactly the same way. Catch-stitch to both shoulder and underarm seams.

1 Front and back neck facings joined at seams

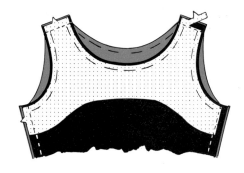

Facing cut in one with garment

2 Facing stitched to neck edge with seam graded and clipped

3 Facing understitched to prevent it from rolling

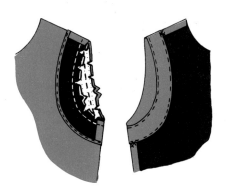

Three stages of applying armhole facing

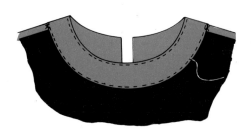

4 Sew facing to interfacing and catchstitch to shoulder seams

Collars and Cuffs

There are three types of collar for which you need to know the basic sewing techniques – the Peter Pan, the convertible shirt collar and the Mandarin or bias-cut collar.
All three types are interfaced.

Peter Pan collar

To make up. Pin and baste the interfacing fabric to the wrong side of the undercollar. Stitch both upper and lower sections of the collar together, leaving the neck edge open.

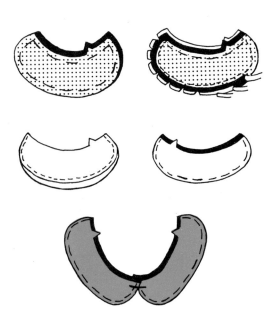

The Peter Pan collar

Turn collar to the right side. Pin and tack the undercollar to the neck edge, right sides of fabric facing. Stitch along neck seam line. Grade seams and clip into curve (see page 36). Turn under the seam allowance on the upper collar and baste then stitch invisibly to the inside neck along the stitched seam line.

Shirt or convertible collar

To make up. In some patterns, the collar and undercollar are cut in one piece but in shaped collars the collar is cut in two pieces, an upper and a lower piece with interfacing between. Make up the collar leaving the neck edge open. Pin and baste the collar to the neck edge. Stitch the front facing to the back facing piece at the shoulder seams. Pin the facing to the neck edge over the collar, right sides together. Baste and then stitch the entire neck edge. Trim interfacing, grade seam allowances and clip into curve (see page 36). Turn facing to the inside, press and catch-stitch to the shoulder seam allowances, leaving the facing free of the garment everywhere else.

Mandarin or bias-cut collar

This type of collar is interfaced with a

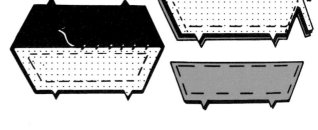

1 Interfacing hemmed to fold line of bodice and stitched to shoulder seams.

2 Making up the collar

3 Collar basted to neck edge

4 Facing pinned to neck edge over collar

5 Grade seam allowances and clip seam

6 Catchstitch facing to shoulder seam allowance

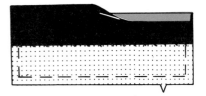

7 Trim interfacing to edge of facing

Mandarin or bias-cut collar: interfacing basted in position and seam allowance turned under firm woven fabric cut with the grain the same way as the top fabric. A non-woven interfacing should not be used. Baste the interfacing to the wrong side of the collar piece. Stitch and then trim the interfacing close to the stitching. Press under the seam allowance on one long edge. Fold the collar in half and stitch both short ends. Turn collar to right side and with right sides facing, pin and tack the folded edge of the collar to the garment, matching notches. Make sure that the centre back edges are evenly matched. Stitch collar to neckline edge. Trim seam allowance of the garment to $\frac{1}{4}$ inch, and that of the collar to $\frac{3}{8}$ inch. Press the seam towards the collar. Turn the seam allowance on the other long edge of the collar under and slip-stitch to the inside of the garment.

Cuffs

There are many ways of finishing off the cuff edges of sleeves. The easiest is a simple bias binding or an applied self-fabric facing. The most difficult for a beginner to attempt is the button-fastened cuff on a gathered sleeve. The technique for this type of cuff is given here:

1. Reinforce the opening to be slashed or clipped on the lower sleeve edge with stay stitching or with facing.

Reinforce slash with stay-stitching

2. Cut a strip of the same fabric the length of the entire slash and two inches wide. Open the slash and spread it until the stay stitching is in a straight line.

Open slash until stitching is straight and stitch fabric to opening

3. Pin the strip of fabric to the opening, right sides together. Stitch $\frac{1}{4}$ inch from the edge, tapering towards the end of the slash. Turn under the free edge of the strip and hem to the seamline.

Hem free edge of strip to seamline

4. Gather the sleeve edge as instructed.

Two rows of basting at lower edge of sleeve

5. Make up the cuff using the same method as that employed for the bias-cut collar.

A beautifully finished cuff

Pin notched edge to sleeve

Hem free edge over seam

6. Attach the cuff to the sleeve, working from the inside first and finishing on the right side with top stitching. Make buttonholes and attach buttons.

The one-piece quick cuff

This is a simple one-piece cuff which can be made for a long sleeve if a stretch fabric such as jersey is being used. Cut the cuff fabric to the measurement of the circumference of the clenched hand plus one inch and by twice the required depth. Right sides facing, join the narrow ends. Turn to the right side and fold double into a cuff. Slip onto the sleeve, raw edges together and right sides facing. Machine stitch $\frac{1}{2}$ inch from the edge. Trim the seam to $\frac{1}{4}$ inch and neaten with zigzag machine stitching. Fold down, the cuff with the seam allowance inside the sleeve.

Setting in sleeves

The traditional technique for sleeves, which used to be taught, involved shrinking the fabric of the head of the sleeve to fit the armhole. Now that so many dressmaking fabrics are pre-shrunk, this method does not work very well and the fullness at the top of the sleeve is 'eased' into the armhole.

Step-by-step guide to setting in a sleeve.

1. Turn the bodice section inside out. Turn the completed sleeve right side out. Slip the sleeve into the garment so that the raw edges of the sleeve and the armhole are matched together on the seamline. Put in a pin or two to hold the sleeve in position.

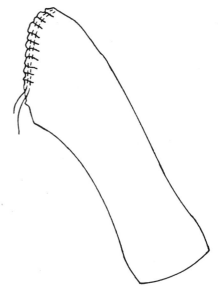

The sleeve made up and gathering stitches drawn up

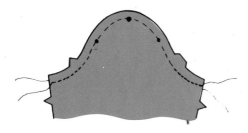

Gathering stitches run on seam line

2. Check to make absolutely sure that you have the right sleeve for the armhole. The back of the armhole is usually marked with two notches which correspond with two notches on the sleeve.

3. Pin and then baste the underarm section as far as the notches on front and back. There is not any ease on this part.

4. The head of the sleeve will have been gathered according to pattern instructions. Hold the bodice in the left hand with the inside of the sleeve towards you. Pin the centre of the sleeve head to the shoulder seam. Then proceed to put in pins, working to both left and right, placing pins across the seamline. Whilst holding the bodice and the sleeve in your left

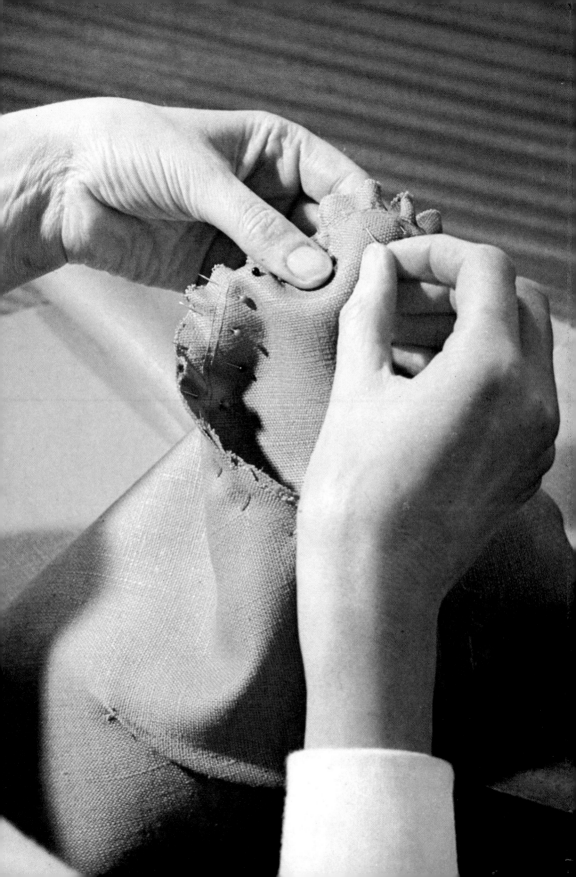

hand, your fingers will make a curved shape similar to the curve of a shoulder and this, you will find, makes it easier to place the pins so that the fullness is properly distributed. Use plenty of pins, as many as you need.

5. Baste all round the sleeve seam firmly and leave a few pins in position during machine stitching to make sure that the fabric does not slip.

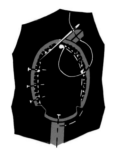

Sleeve pinned and basted into bodice

6. Pull the sleeve through the armhole and machine stitch, working from the sleeve side of the seam. Two rows of machining is advisable. Trim

the underarm seam allowance to $\frac{1}{4}$ inch and oversew to neaten.

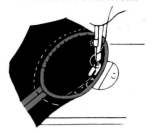

Machine stitch with sleeve uppermost

Two-piece set-in sleeve

The two-piece sleeve, featured on the Chanel-type suit, pattern No. 17 is made up in two sections, both of which are shaped so that the finished sleeve fits without the use of darts. Join the two sections with plain seams and then insert the sleeve into the armhole in the same way as for a one-piece sleeve. Cuff edges are finished off in a suitable way, either with a single hem, a bias-cut facing or with bias binding cut from the same fabric.

Setting a sleeve into an armhole

Waistbands

The waistline of fitted skirts and trousers can be finished off in one of three simple ways – with a self-fabric waistband, with an interfaced facing or with a petersham band.

The waistband should lap front over back on a side closing and left over right on a back closing. After the zip has been inserted, close the waistband with two hooks and eyes or with a worked buttonhole and a button.

Self-fabric waistband

A waistband is usually cut along the lengthwise grain to prevent it from stretching. Interfacing is cut to half the depth of the band.

To make up. Turn under the seam allowance on the long edge of the waistband piece that has no notches. Pin and baste the interfacing to the

Interfacing hemmed to foldline

wrong side of the fabric, matching the notched edges and with the other edge of the interfacing along what will be the fold line.

Catch the interfacing to the fold line. Pin the notched edge of the waistband to the waist of the skirt, notches

Stitch on seamline and grade seams

Stitch waistband ends, trim and grade seams

Lap free edge on waistband seam and pin

matching and right sides facing. Baste while easing the waistband onto the skirt. Stitch.

Trim interfacing close to stitching. Grade seams.

Press seam towards waistband. Fold the waistband, right sides facing and stitch the short ends.

Turn to the right side and press. Hem the folded edge of the waistband to the seamline on the inside of the skirt.

Hem waistband to seamline on inside

Hooks are sewn to the overlap of the closing

Faced waistband

Work following the same method given for applying facings (see page 42).

Petersham bands

Cut petersham ribbon to the waist measurement plus $2\frac{1}{2}$ inches.

Make a 1-inch hem on each of the short ends.

Pin and baste the petersham to the waistline on the right side of the fabric, making a small pleat, approximately $\frac{1}{8}$ inch at the side, the centre front and centre back for ease. The petersham should be standing up above the skirt edge.

Stitch $\frac{1}{8}$ inch from the edge of the ribbon. Turn the ribbon inside the skirt and press. Sew hook and eye fastenings to the hemmed ends.

Waist plackets

A placket is the opening in a seam simply to allow one to get in and out of a garment easily. Never alter the recommended depth of a placket as this could make the skirt difficult to slide over the hips. Most plackets are closed with a zip fastener but occasionally a pattern will recommend that hooks and eyes be used.

Fastenings

The fastenings on your hand-made clothes – zips, buttons, buttonholes, press studs, hooks and eyes – must be beautifully done if the finished garments are to have the professional look which is the aim of every dress-maker. There are special techniques for sewing fastenings and you should learn these right from the start.

Zip fasteners

Zip fasteners are made both in nylon and metal and come in different weights for different types of clothes. They can be bought with an open end for the front of a jacket and a curved type is available for trouser fly fastenings. The leading brands mark their packets clearly with the type of garment for which the zip is intended. Zips are manufactured in a very wide range of colours but if an exact match is difficult to achieve, buy one that is near enough the right colour, and in a lighter tone rather than a dark tone.

Make sure that you buy a zip long enough for the opening and if necessary, make the opening longer to fit the nearest sized zip. The stop at the bottom of the zip should be exactly level with the bottom of the opening so that there is no strain on the lowest teeth of the zip when the garment is being put on and taken off. For back fastenings, the top of the zip should be about $\frac{1}{2}$ inch below the neck edge and a hook and eye should be sewn about it to take the strain off the top teeth.

Stitch the zip in by machine, if your machine has a zipper foot, otherwise sew zips in by hand. Use pick stitch (see page 32) to do this and the stitches will be both strong and invisible. It is a wise precaution to neaten the turnings of the opening before putting the zip in because threads can very easily catch in zips and make them stick.

Follow the instructions on the packet for the best method of inserting a zip.

Three kinds of buttonholes are used in dressmaking – bound buttonholes, hand worked and eyelet buttonholes. A perfectly adequate buttonhole can be worked on swing needle sewing machines using the zigzag stitch and the machine manufacturer's handbook will give instructions for making this.

Bound buttonholes

Bound buttonholes must be made on interfaced areas of the garment.

Zip fasteners are both practical and decorative (Photograph by Lightning Zip Fasteners Ltd)

The method is as follows:

1. Cut a piece of fabric on the lengthwise grain 2 inches deep and to the width of the finished buttonhole plus $\frac{1}{2}$ inch.

2. Fold lengthwise and crease. Baste in position on the right side of fabric with the crease lying on the button-hole mark. Mark the width of the buttonhole along the crease with basting stitches.

3. Stitch with very small stitches round the marked line, $\frac{1}{8}$ inch away from it, along both sides and along each end.

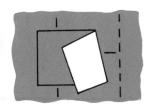 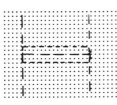

4. With sharp, pointed scissors, cut the fabric along the basted line to within $\frac{1}{8}$ inch of each end of the buttonhole and then into the corners.

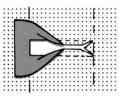 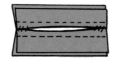

5. Turn the fabric through the slit to the wrong side (see diagram) to form a narrow binding on both edges of the

buttonhole and square the ends off neatly with a small pleat.

6. Baste flat and press.

7. Neaten by sewing all round the edge of the buttonhole on the right side, using pick stitches.

8. On the wrong side, baste the facing in position, cut a slit in the facing to correspond with the buttonhole, turn in the edges and hem neatly to the back of the buttonhole fabric.

Handworked buttonholes

Handworked buttonholes take rather a long time to do and need a great deal of patience but if you are making a garment from an expensive or a very lightweight fabric, then they are well worth the effort. They are also suitable for fabrics such as tweeds where bound buttonholes cannot be worked easily.

Two stages of the worked buttonhole

Handworked buttonholes are worked after the facing has been completed. Mark the position of the buttonhole and outline it with small stitches. Cut the slit through the fabric, interfacing and facing with a sharp, pointed pair of scissors.

Over-sew the cut edges immediately if the fabric frays easily. Work buttonhole stitch round the slit, starting from the square end. When you have stitched round the rounded end, using satin stitch on the curve instead of buttonhole stitch, finish by making three or four straight stitches across the square end and then buttonhole stitch across them.

Eyelet buttonholes

Cut a small circle with a stiletto and outline the circle with small running stitches. Work buttonhole stitch all round the edge closely.

Loop fastenings

Loop fastenings can be made of fabric or of thread, the former being a decorative form of fastening and the latter purely functional. Fabric loops are stitched into position before the facing is applied.

Thread loops

Use either buttonhole twist thread or pure silk.

To work: Sew two or three strands of thread through the fabric to the depth of the intended loop. Work over these threads with buttonhole stitch. If the loop is right on the edge of the garment and is to be used for a ball button, it helps to slip a matchstick under the threads while the buttonhole stitching is being worked.

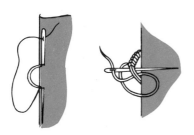

Thread loops

Fabric loops

Making the rouleau. Rouleau is the term given to a narrow tube of fabric. To make this, cut a strip of bias-cut fabric the width of the finished tube plus seam allowance. $1\frac{1}{4}$ inches is

usually enough. Fold in half lengthwise, right sides together and stitch leaving the ends open. Fasten a strong thread to one end of the tube at the seam. Using a bodkin or a large-eyed needle, and pushing it eye first through the tube, pull the thread through. This will turn the tube inside out. Do not press.

Making rouleau from bias strips

Making the loops. Cut the rouleau to the correct length to fit over the button plus seam allowances. Make the size and spacing of the loops on a piece of paper and sew the loops to the paper.

Stitch the loops, still on the paper, in position on the right side of the garment edge. Tear the paper away, apply the facing. Stitch the buttons to match the loops.

Stages of making loop fastenings

Snap fasteners

Snaps are used as fasteners where there is not likely to be very much strain but where a closure is needed. Stitch fasteners fairly close together,

about an inch apart if very small,
2 inches if they are fairly large. The
ball part of the fastener goes on to the
overlapping fabric.

To work. Fasten the thread to the
spot where the fastener is going to be
with a double back stitch. Hold the
fastener down with the left thumb
and stitch through each hole in turn
with four or five buttonhole stitches.

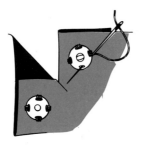

Take the thread under the snap to go
from one hole to the next. The
stitches should go through the fabric
and the interfacing but should not
show on the right side of the garment.
Sew the socket part of the fastener in
the same way.
For a couture finish, if the fasteners
are rather large, cover both parts

with circles of matching silk fabric
gathered round the edges before
sewing them on. The ball will break
through the silk and make a hole in
the socket the first time the fastener
is closed.

Hooks and eyes

Hooks and eyes are used mostly as a
waistband fastening.
The hook part is stitched to the
overlap about $\frac{1}{8}$ inch from the edge of
the opening and buttonhole stitches
are used to secure the fastener to the
fabric. Make stitches all round the

holes of the hook and straight
stitches across the end under the
hook. Round eyes are stitched so
that they extend just beyond the edge
of the garment opening. Bar eyes are
placed about $\frac{1}{8}$ inch in from the edge.

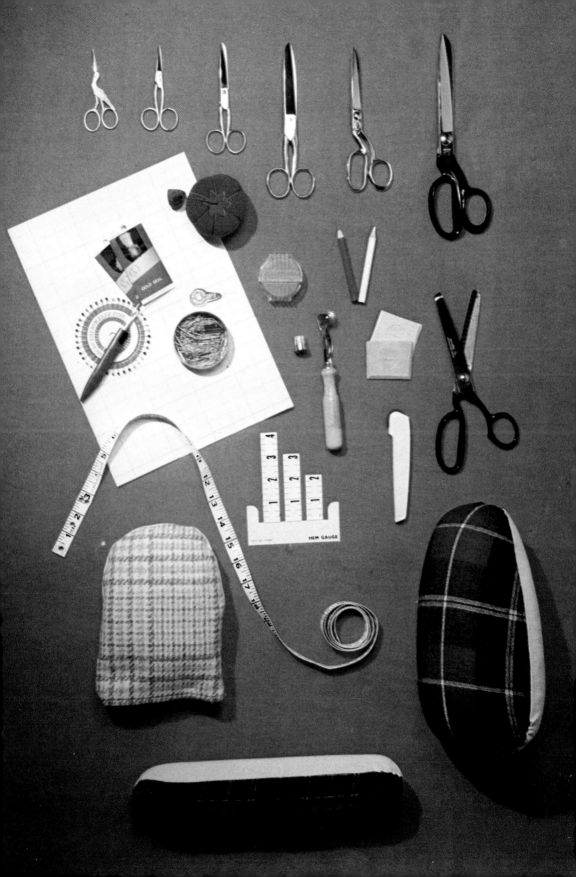

Perfect hems

The last perfect touch to an immaculately made garment is the hemline – and it is particularly important in those styles where the hemline area is the fashion point. Here are some basic rules for making hemlines:

1. Get someone else to measure while you are wearing the garment, measuring upwards from the floor.
2. Sew the garment working with it flat on the table so that the weight is supported.
3. Trim the raw edge if necessary to neaten before pinning up.
4. Pin evenly, placing pins at right angles to the hem. Never slant pins or the fabric may be pulled out of its true line. As you pin, the fabric will flute between the pins.
5. Baste about $2\frac{1}{2}$ inches from the folded edge and then press the fluted edge lightly with a damp cloth to shrink out the flutes. Do not press too hard or marks may be made through the fabric to the right side.
6. Baste again, $\frac{1}{2}$ inch down from the raw edge.
7. Hold the full depth of the hem in your hand and without creasing it

turn under a $\frac{1}{4}$ inch hem on the raw edge and stitch with invisible stitch (See page 33). Pick up only two or

Press along basted edge

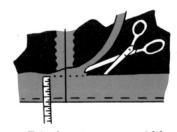

Trim hem to an even width

three threads from the skirt fabric and more fabric from the hem itself. Leave a loop every three or four stitches for ease.
8. Remove basting stitches and press again.

The pretty touch

Hand-made clothes can look delightful and rather expensive if you take the trouble to add decorative details. These can be as simple as neatly made loop fastenings or pretty buttons. Lace edgings and inserts give a charming feminine air to fragile clothes and pin tucks, worked on a baby's dress, are a lovely way to do fine needlework.

Braid and ribbon, stitched round the edges of a suit jacket or the hem of a full skirt add a distinctive touch. Ruffles, while requiring a little patience to make, lend a great deal of glamour to lingerie and nightdresses. Narrow ruffles, sewn in rows, look very dramatic on long, full sleeves. Embroidery on clothes can convey any expression or mood. Small flower motifs, for instance, look pretty scattered across the bodice of a garment, while personal monograms and initials look smart on pockets, lapels and personal accessories. Formal cross-stitched designs look attractive down sleeves or in bands round skirt hems; children's clothes, as well as adults', can be decorated with bands of smocking.

Wool embroidery looks effective on fashion clothes, too. Big, bold flowers in brilliant colours worked on wool fabrics can look marvellous. The possibilities in embroidery are endless.

Embroidery should always be worked on garment sections before making them up.

Appliqué

To apply motifs to garments, trace off the design and transfer it to the contrasting fabric. Machine stitch round the outline of the motif. Cut out the shape allowing $\frac{1}{8}$ inch round the outside of the machine stitching. Turn this allowance under on the stitched line, press and baste to the garment. Hem or blanket stitch in position.

An alternative method for appliqué is worked on a swing needle sewing machine. Cut out the motif with a $\frac{1}{4}$-inch margin all round. Baste to the garment in position and machine stitch $\frac{1}{4}$ inch from the edge on the seamline. Trim the fabric off close to the machine stitching. Work close zigzag stitch all round, covering the raw edges.

Braids, ribbons and ric-rac

Braids and ribbons can be applied by hand or by machine. Narrow widths will need only one row of stitches down the centre while wider braids and ribbons will require stitching along both edges.

Ruffles

Ruffled edging can be purchased ready-made and this is simply stitched to the garment along the firm edge.

To make ruffles, allow fabric about twice to three times the finished length of the ruffle. Sheer or fine fabrics need more fullness than heavy ones. Bias-cut ruffles hang better but for an edging on skirts or aprons, the fabric can be cut to either lengthwise or crosswise grain.

Most sewing machines have an attachment for sewing a narrow hem on ruffles but if you prefer to do it by hand, roll and hem the edge. Divide and mark the hemmed fabric into quarters and gather evenly between the marks. This can be done either by hand or by machine, using a large-sized stitch. Stitch two rows and leave the ends of the threads free for adjustments to gathers.

To attach a ruffle

Faced ruffles. This method of application is used on faced edges such as collars or within a seam for an edging.
Draw up the ruffle. Pin the gathered edge to the edge of the garment, right sides facing. Match seamlines. Allow more fullness at corners. Baste. Pin facing right side down over the ruffle, matching seamlines. Baste and then stitch through all thicknesses. Trim corners, grade seams. Turn to the right side.

As a hem finish. Use this method of application where there is no facing such as on a hem.
Pin the edge of the ruffle to the garment edge, right sides facing, matching seamlines. Baste a strip of bias fabric right side down over the ruffle. Stitch on the seamline. Trim seam. Hem the other edge of the bias down to cover the raw edges of the garment and the ruffle.

Lace edgings

Lace edging should always be sewn on by hand for a delicate look. Use a sharp needle and fine thread. Place lace edge against the finished edge of the fabric, right sides facing and join the edges with oversewing or whipping stitch. Mitre the corners as illustrated by folding the lace down at the corner and cutting away the excess fabric. Sew the cut edges together with oversewing.

Lace insert

This is a very simple way of applying insert lace to a garment. Baste the lace, which has two straight edges, in position on the wrong side of the fabric. On the right side, cut away the fabric over the lace leaving $\frac{3}{8}$ inch on either side for turnings. Turn the

Flower-pretty embroidery; trace pattern on page 65 (Photograph by J & P Coats Ltd)

62

raw edges under to make narrow hems and machine stitch to the lace.

Embroidered bolero for a little girl

To work the embroidery on a bolero, trace off the design, which is given life-size. Trace the design down onto the fabric using dressmaker's carbon paper and reversing the tracing for the opposite side of the bolero.

Diagram 1 gives the key to stitches and colours of thread.

Materials required:

Child's bolero, made of a smooth fabric or of felt.

Clark's Anchor Stranded Cotton in the following colours and quantities: Muscat Green 0280 2 skeins; Rose Madder 056 1 skein; Cyclamen 085, 088 1 skein each; Jade 0186, 0189 1 skein each; Muscat Green 0278 1 skein.

Crewel needle No. 8.

To work, use two strands of thread throughout. All parts of the design similar to numbered parts are worked in the same colour and stitch.

Press completed embroidery on the wrong side.

1 – 056		
2 – 085		
3 – 088		
4 – 0186	}	Satin Stitch
5 – 0189		
6 – 0278		
7 – 0280		
8 – 056		
9 – 085		
10 – 088	}	French Knots
11 – 0186		
12 – 0189		
13 – 0280		
14 – 0189		
15 – 0278	}	Stem Stitch
16 – 0280		
17 – 0186	}	Back Stitch
18 – 0189		
19 – 088 – Double Knot Stitch		
20 – 0189 – Buttonhole Stitch		

Diagram 1 – key to stitches and threads

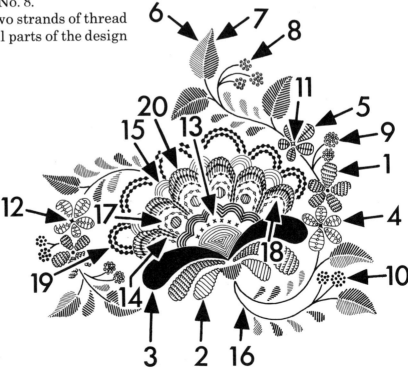

64

Trace pattern for the girl's bolero embroidery

Making a paper pattern

Here is a complete wardrobe of patterns for you to make up with the dressmaking know-how you have acquired. The patterns are given as graph patterns and these can seem rather strange at first. In fact, they are worked out in exactly the same way as commercial paper patterns but are scaled down to fit on to the page. The only difference is that a graph pattern is a plan from which you make your own paper pattern. Graph patterns can be very useful because while you are drawing out, minor alterations can be made to size, the style can be changed or fit can be improved. All the adults' graph patterns are given in one size only – size 12, 34 inch bust – to maintain clarity and to make them easier to understand. These and the children's patterns can be adapted to a size smaller and up to two sizes larger (see page 15).

1 Quick-make hostess apron
2 Apron for a man
3 Long gathered skirt
4 Sleeveless long evening dress
5 A-line button-through skirt
6 Short nightdress
7 Short housecoat
8 Angel top for a baby
9 Baby's sleeping bag
10 Trousers and waistcoat for a teenager
11 Top and trousers for a child
12 Pleated dress for a little girl
13 Short sleeved dress for a little girl
14 Baby's play trousers
15 Pinafore dress
16 Long-sleeved classic blouse
17 Chanel-type two piece suit
18 Trouser suit
19 Pleated skirt

To make a paper pattern from a graph pattern you will need the following materials and equipment.

Squared paper. This can be obtained from the dress fabric department of some large stores and is quite inexpensive. The sheets measure 30 inches by 20 inches, and they need to be joined together for patterns with several garment pieces.

If you cannot obtain squared paper, branches of chain stationers sell graph paper which will do just as well, but it is a little more expensive and the sheets are not as large.

Ruler. Ideally, one should use a yardstick measuring 36 inches long for pattern drafting but an ordinary 12-inch rule can be used, together with a tape measure.

Pencils. Medium-soft pencils, B or 2B are best. A black felt-tipped pen is also required for strengthening the lines of the master pattern.

Eraser for correcting mistakes
Sellotape or Scotch tape for joining pattern sheets.
Scissors – a sharp pair kept especially for paper
Tracing paper. Buy a roll of tracing paper if you decide to keep your master pattern for re-use. Trace the pattern pieces off on to the tracing paper.

Drawing out the pattern

1. Check the scale given on the graph patterns. All those here are 1 inch to 1 square, which means that every square on the graph represents a 1 inch square on your squared paper. [The squared paper will be marked off into 1-inch squares with a heavy line.]
2. Number the graph pattern squares across the top and then down the side.
3. Draw out the area of the graph pattern on the squared paper and number in the same way.
4. You have now reproduced the area you are going to work in, scaled up from the graph pattern.

5. Draw the straight lines in first, for instance the line marked 'FOLD'. Look at the sample given here and you will see that in square 1 across and 2 down the line curves upwards.
6. Mark the places where the line of the pattern touches the lines of the graph as dots on your squared paper. When all the dots showing the outline of a piece have been marked, join them up. If the line looks a bit uneven, rub out and re-draw a smooth line.
7. Draw out all the pieces in the same way.
8. Mark in very carefully all the marks and words on the pattern pieces. You have now made your master pattern.

If you have decided to increase or decrease the size of the pattern this is the point at which it should be done. If the master pattern is to be kept for re-use, trace off all the pieces on to tracing paper and make sure that all words and markings are traced off also. If the master pattern is not intended to be kept, it is now cut out ready for pinning to the fabric.

A seam allowance of $\frac{5}{8}$ inch has been included on all patterns throughout the book.

NOTE: Dotted lines on the graph pattern indicate where patterns may be lengthened or shortened.

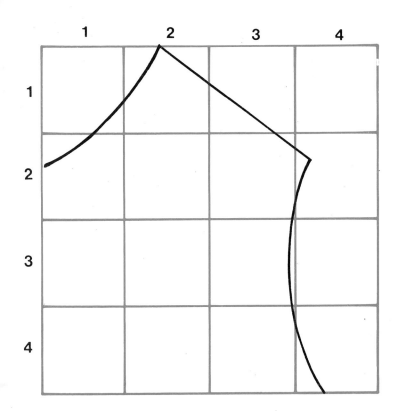

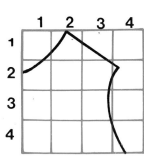

1. Mark numbers against the squares along one side and across the top of the graph pattern.

2. Tape dressmaker's squared paper together so that you have sufficient for the pattern. Number the pattern paper in the same way as the graph pattern.

3. Draw in any straight lines running vertically or horizontally first.

4. Following the graph pattern, mark dots on the lines of your pattern paper to correspond exactly with the places where the line of the pattern falls on the lines of the graph.

5. Join up the dots, following the curves of the pattern on the graph.

6. Write in all words and numerals; mark all balance marks.

Quick-make apron

No pattern is required for this apron – the pieces are simply cut to size.

Make it full-length for an apron glamorous enough to greet your guests in and add a 3-inch ruffle to the hem for a pretty look.

Materials required:

1 yard 36-inch wide fabric (for short version)
2½ yards will be required for a long apron.
Coats bias binding.
Coats Drima thread

Cutting directions

½ inch has been included for seam allowance.
Main section – 1 piece, 19 inches deep by 36 inches wide
Ties – 2 pieces, 4 inches deep by 38 inches wide.
Waistband – 1 piece, 5 inches deep by 20 inches wide.

To make up

1. Bind one long and two short edges of the main section.

2. Make two rows of gathering stitches along the seam line on the remaining edge of the main section.

3. Turn in the seam allowance on both short ends of the waistband and baste.

4. Place the gathered edge of the main section to the long edge of the waistband, matching seam lines, right sides together. Baste and stitch.

5. Fold the waistband and turn under the remaining raw edge. Baste to the seam line along the stitching.

6. Baste and stitch ¼-inch hems on the long edges and on one short end of both ties.

7. Insert the raw end of the ties into the open end of the waistband pleating to fit. Baste to secure.

8. Top-stitch the waistband all round, ⅛ inch from the edge, through all thicknesses of fabric.

For the longer version, cut the main piece 36 inches wide by 60 inches deep and do not bind the edges. Cut and join strips 4 inches deep to make a strip 90 inches wide for the ruffle. Turn a narrow hem on the two sides of the main section and make up and add the ruffle to the hem.

Apron for a man

Make this smart, hard-wearing apron for a domestically minded man and, if he is the type, add an appliqué motif to the pocket – a carrot shape, for instance, or a design of crossed spoons. In a plain fabric, the same pattern would make a gardening apron.

Materials required:
1¼ yards 36-inch wide fabric
Coats Drima thread.
Scraps of fabric for appliqué motif if required.

Cutting directions
Make a paper pattern from the graph pattern.
⅝ inch seam allowance included.
Pattern A – cut 1.
Pocket – 1 piece, 10 inches by 8½ inches.
Neckband – 1 piece, 2¼ inches by 21 inches.
Ties – 2 pieces, 2¼ inches by 30 inches

To make up
1. Fold the neckband in half lengthwise, right sides together. Baste and then stitch along the long edges. Turn to the right side.
2. Make up the ties in the same way, stitching along the long edges and one short end. Leave one short end of each tie open.
3. Turn a narrow hem on all sides of the main apron piece and machine stitch.
4. Turn a narrow hem on both ends of the neckband and press flat. Pin to the upper edge of the apron, at the corners so that the folded edge is about half an inch below the edge of the apron. Baste and then machine stitch the neckband to the apron.
5. Stitch ties to each side of the apron in the same way.
6. To neaten pocket edge, turn in ¼ inch on one short edge and stitch. Fold again 1½ inches to make a facing. Turn remaining edges to the wrong side, press and baste. Topstitch to apron.

Graph pattern for a man's apron

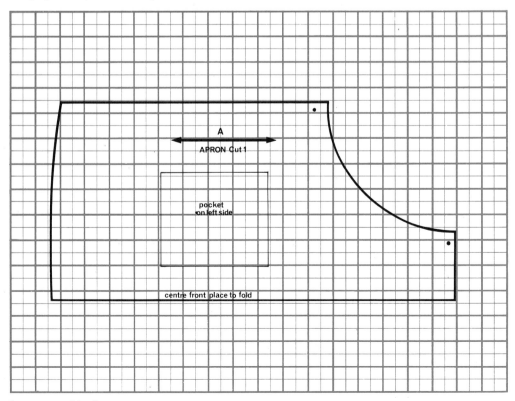

A

APRON Cut 1

pocket
on left side

centre front place to fold

1 square = 1 inch

Hostess skirt

Here is another simple garment that does not require a pattern to make it. The skirt can be made to fit any waist and hip measurement and the fabric quantities given here make a skirt $41\frac{1}{2}$ inches long from waist to hem.

An alternative way to use the pattern might be to make the skirt up in a light summer fabric, cutting the length short to the knee, or in a plain fabric, trimming the hem with bands of ric-rac braid in bright, contrasting colours.

Materials required:

$1\frac{1}{3}$ yards of 54-inch wide fabric.
Interfacing for the waistband.
8-inch zip fastener.
2 hooks and eyes.
Coats Drima thread.

Cutting directions

$\frac{5}{8}$ inch has been included for seam allowance.
Skirt – 1 piece, 44 inches by 54 inches.

Waistband – 1 piece, $5\frac{3}{4}$ inches by the waist measurement plus $2\frac{3}{4}$ inches.
Waistband interlining – 1 piece $2\frac{7}{8}$ inches by the waist measurement plus $2\frac{3}{4}$ inches.

To make up

1. Fold skirt piece to make a piece 27 inches by 44 inches, baste and stitch the long edges together, leaving one end unstitched $8\frac{3}{4}$ inches for inserting the zip.
2. Insert the zip fastener. This is the Centre Back of the Skirt.
3. Make two rows of gathering stitches along the waistline seam line. Pull up the gathers to the waist measurement.
4. Make up the waistband with the interfacing and stitch to the waist of the Skirt.
5. Sew hooks and eyes to the waistband.
6. Make a hem on the lower edge. Give a final pressing and neaten all seams.

Hostess skirt

Evening dress

A sleeveless, high-necked dress which will have a favourite place in your wardrobe because it is a classic – and timeless.
Make it up in any fabric which pleases you. The pattern will also adapt to make a sleeveless and very pretty blouse to wear under suits. Simply cut the pattern short 4 inches below the waist and use a shorter zip. The neckline can be given a different look by making up a soft bow and stitching it to the front of the collar or by cutting an extra length of fabric to make a scarf, stitching it to one side of the back fastening and allowing it to drape over one shoulder. The collar can be heavily beaded for a really glamorous look.

Materials required:

3¼ yards 45-inch wide fabric
Interfacing for collar.
22-inch zip fastener.
2 hooks and eyes.
Coats Drima thread.

Cutting directions

Make a paper pattern from the graph pattern, 1 square = 1 inch. ⅝ inch seam allowance has been included.

Long evening dress

Pattern A - Front cut 1 piece, facing cut off right side.
Pattern B – Back cut 2 facing cut off right side.
Pattern C – Armhole facing cut 2.
Pattern D – Collar cut 2, one from fabric, one from interfacing.

To make up

1. Baste and stitch darts on Front and Back.
2. Baste and stitch Centre Back seam, leaving 22 inches of seam unstitched for inserting zip fastener.
3. Join shoulder seams and right side seam.
4. Baste and stitch Back to Front at left seam to top of facing.
5. Insert zip fastener at Centre Back seam.
6. Make up and attach interfaced collar.
7. Sew hooks and eyes to fasten collar at back.
8. Baste and stitch armhole facings seams. Place facings to armholes, right sides facing, baste, stitch and trim. Turn to the inside of the dress. Catch facing to dress at shoulder and side seams.
9. Turn up and make the hem.
10. Turn side slit facings to the wrong side and sew lightly in position with catch-stitches.

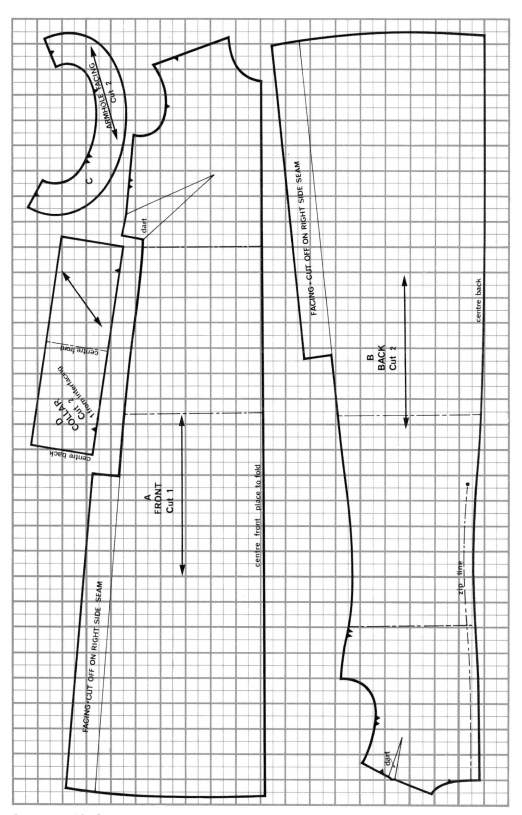

ARMHOLE FACING
Cut 2

C

dart

D
COLLAR
Cut 2
1 from interfacing

centre front

centre back

A
FRONT
Cut 1

centre front place to fold

FACING · CUT OFF ON RIGHT SIDE SEAM

FACING · CUT OFF ON RIGHT SIDE SEAM

B
BACK
Cut 2

centre back

zip line

dart

1 square = 1 inch

77

Simple skirt

A neat A-line skirt with a buttoned front fastening for casual wear, finished with contrast coloured top-stitching for fashion detail.

The buttonholes on the skirt illustrated were worked on a swing-needle sewing machine using the zigzag stitch, but if preferred, work bound buttonholes. The pattern can be adapted to a classic side-fastening skirt by omitting the front facings from the pattern and adding $\frac{5}{8}$ inch seam allowance to each side of centre front. Leave the left side seam open and insert a zip fastener. Make an interfaced waistband to finish.

Materials required:

$1\frac{5}{8}$ yards 54-inch wide fabric.
Interfacing for facings and waistband.
Seven 1-inch wide buttons.
Coats Drima thread.
Pearl Cotton No. 8 for top-stitching.

Cutting directions

Make a paper pattern from the graph pattern, 1 square = 1 inch. $\frac{5}{8}$ inch seam allowances have been included.
Pattern A – Front cut 2
Pattern B – Back cut 1
Pattern C – Front waist facing cut 4, (2 from interfacing)

Pattern D – Back waist facing cut 4, (2 from interfacing)
Front facings – cut 2 strips from interfacing, 2 inches by Centre Front measurement

To make up

1. Baste and stitch back and front darts.
2. Baste front interfacings to wrong side of front sections.
3. Baste and stitch Skirt Fronts and Skirt Backs at side seams.
4. Baste waist interfacings to waist facings.
5. Baste and stitch front facings to back waist facings at side seams.
6. Baste and stitch skirt waist facing to skirt front facings at side seams. Edge stitch remainder of inner edge of facing.
7. Turn facing to outside along fold line. Baste and stitch waist edge. Sew facing lightly to darts and seams.
8. Mitre corners at hem by bringing seam lines right sides together, baste and stitch. Trim seam and turn to the wrong side.
9. Make hem on lower edge.
Make buttonholes on right front of skirt. Sew buttons to correspond.
10. Top stitch $\frac{1}{4}$ inch from skirt edges by winding Pearl cotton No. 8 on bobbin of sewing machine. Thread machine with Drima thread and set machine for longest stitch. Machine from wrong side of fabric.

Graph pattern for A-line skirt

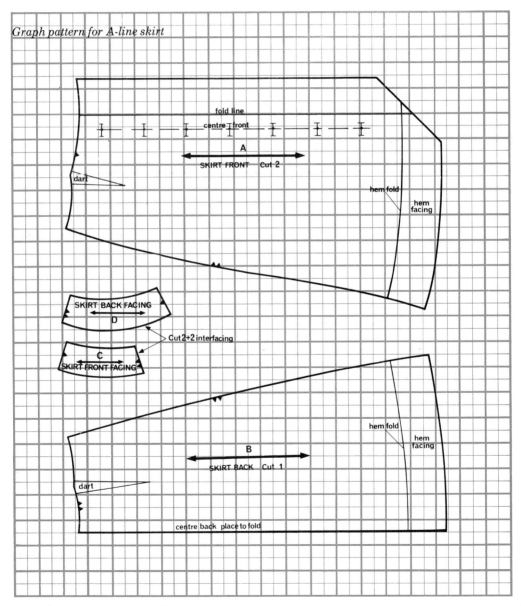

fold line

centre front

A

SKIRT FRONT   Cut 2

dart

hem fold

hem facing

SKIRT BACK FACING

D

Cut 2+2 interfacing

C

SKIRT FRONT FACING

hem fold

hem facing

B

SKIRT BACK   Cut 1

dart

centre back place to fold

1 square = 1 inch

Nightdress

A sweetly pretty nightdress to make from a very simple pattern. The nightdress illustrated was made up in broderie anglaise but an equally pretty effect would be achieved with flowered cotton lawn, dotted Swiss or two layers of Terylene organdie or chiffon. The pattern can be extended very easily to make a full-length nightdress and bias-cut ruffles could be added to the neckline and to the hem.

Materials required:

2¾ yards 45-inch wide fabric.
Coats Drima thread.
(allow 1 yard extra fabric for ruffles).

Cutting directions

Make a paper pattern from the graph pattern

1 square = 1 inch. ⅝ inch seam allowance has been included.
Pattern A – Front cut 1.
Pattern B – Back cut 1
Cut bias strip 1½ inches wide for neck binding, armhole binding and bow and join for length.

To make up

1. Gather neckline edge of Front piece as required.
2. Gather Back piece neckline in the centre for four inches.
3. Join shoulder seams and side seams.
4. Apply bias binding to the neckline, and the armholes.
5. Make rouleau for the front bow and stitch in position.
6. Make the hem.

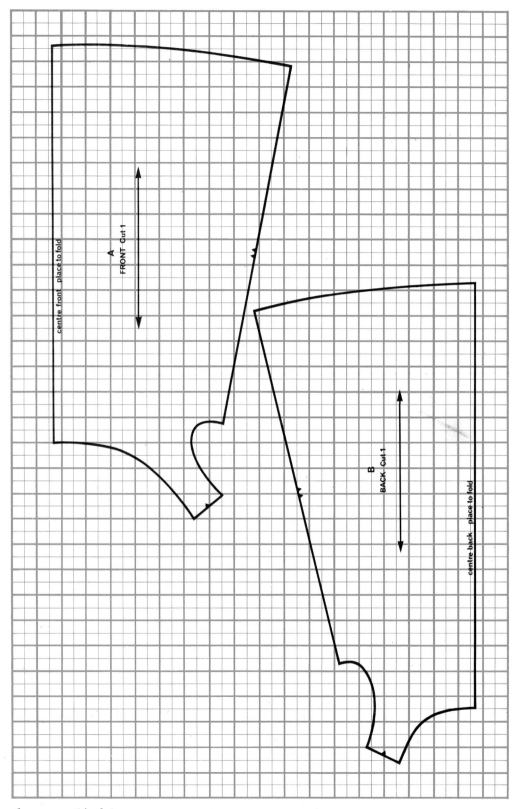

A
FRONT Cut 1

centre front place to fold

B
BACK Cut 1

centre back place to fold

1 square = 1 inch

82

Housecoat

This easy-to-wear raglan-sleeved housecoat can be made up in the same fabric as the nightdress or, as shown, in a contrasting fabric. The pattern makes up equally well in winter-weight fabrics, such as Courtelle, which require no lining.

The housecoat can of course be cut as a full-length garment and if preferred the facings can be left off the pattern and seam allowances added to Centre Front pieces.

A zip fastener closing can then be inserted, either from neckline to hem or simply from neckline to a given point. For this type of fastening, the zip should be open-ended.

Materials required:

4 yards 36-inch wide fabric.
$10 \times \frac{3}{4}$ inch buttons.
Gathered edging if required.
Coats Drima thread.

Cutting directions

Make a paper pattern from the graph pattern
1 square = 1 inch.
$\frac{5}{8}$ inch seam allowance has been included.
Pattern A – Front cut 2
Pattern B – Back cut 2.
Pattern C – Sleeve cut 2.
Pattern D – Back neck facing cut 1.

Pattern E – Pocket cut 2.

To make up

1. Baste and stitch Centre Back seam.
2. Baste and stitch front darts and sleeve shoulder darts.
3. Baste and join front to back at side seams.
4. Baste and stitch sleeve seams.
5. Stitch sleeves to main section. Clip curves so that they lie flat.
6. Stitch shoulder seams of back neck facing to front facing.
7. Fold back facing to outside on fold line. Stitch neck edge. Clip seams and turn to the wrong side. Catch facing to housecoat shoulder darts and sleeve seams.
8. Make hems on sleeves and lower edges.
9. Fold pocket pieces in half, right sides together on fold line. Baste and stitch leaving an opening for turning to right side.
10. Turn to right side and slipstitch opening.
11. Stitch trimming round front and neck edges.
12. Baste trimming to curved pocket edges. Stitch pockets to housecoat fronts.
13. Make buttonholes on right front. Sew buttons on left front to correspond.

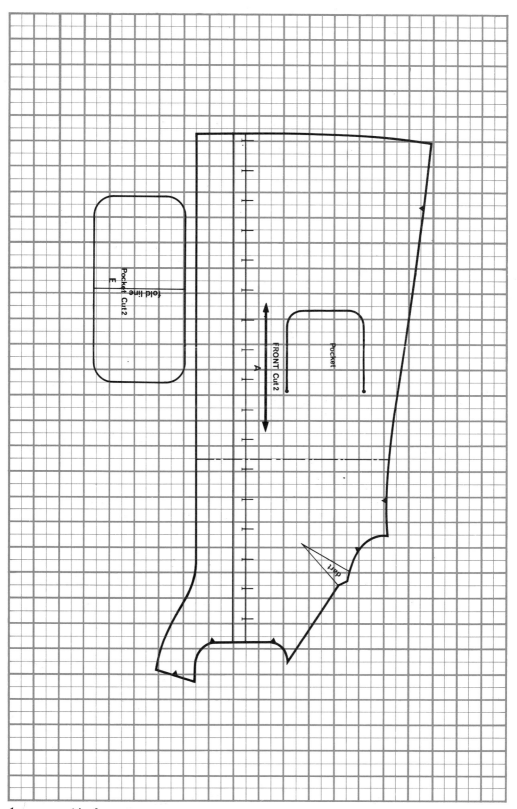

1 square = 1 inch

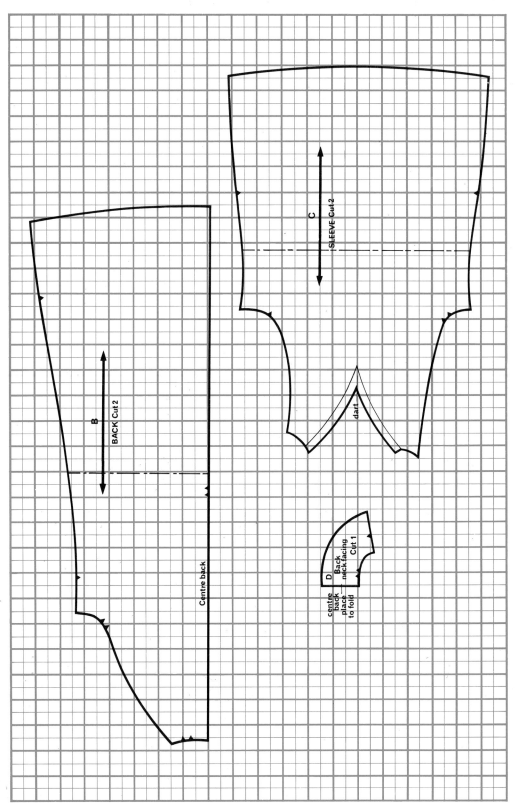

B

BACK Cut 2

Centre back

C

SLEEVE Cut 2

dart

D Back
neck facing
Cut 1

centre
back
place
to fold

1 square = 1 inch

Baby's angel top

A pretty angel top for a six-month-old baby, to sew in light-weight fabrics. French seams would be ideal to give a flat neat seam finish but plain seams can be worked if you prefer.

Materials required:

1 yard 36-inch wide fabric.
$\frac{1}{4}$ yard narrow elastic.
Coats bias binding.
$3 \times \frac{1}{4}$-inch buttons.
Coats Drima thread.

Cutting directions

Make paper pattern from the graph pattern 1 square = 1 inch. $\frac{5}{8}$ inch seam allowances have been included.
Pattern A – Front skirt cut 1.
Pattern B – Back cut 1.
Pattern C – Yoke cut 2

To make up

Pattern D – Sleeve cut 2.
Cut bias strip for finishing off neck edge.
1. Gather yoke seam line on Front skirt between notches.

2. Place right side of one yoke section to wrong side of skirt, matching raw edges. Pull up gathers to fit. Baste.
3. Baste second yoke section, right sides together with raw edges even along gathered edge. Stitch all thicknesses of fabric. Baste yoke sections together.
4. Make a narrow hem on sleeve edges. Make wrist casings with bias binding on the wrong side of the fabric.
5. Cut elastic to baby's wrist measurement plus 1 inch. Insert through casings. Stitch ends to seam allowance of sleeve.
6. To make the back opening, slit from neck edge down the centre of the back skirt to the dot. Make a $\frac{1}{4}$-inch clip at the lower end of the slit. Turn in $\frac{1}{4}$-inch hems on slit edges and stitch.
7. Press stitched edges to inside along fold line and sew in place. Overlap right opening edge over left to form a pleat below the opening. Stitch through all thicknesses at end of slit.
8. Baste sleeves to front and back sections, right sides together. Stitch then clip curves.
9. Baste and stitch front to back along entire underarm and side seams.

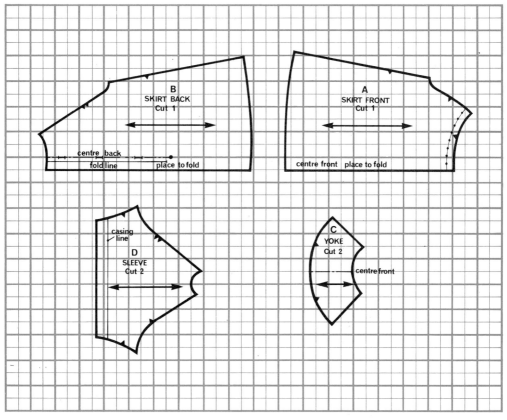

B
SKIRT BACK
Cut 1

centre back
fold line   place to fold

A
SKIRT FRONT
Cut 1

centre front   place to fold

casing
line
D
SLEEVE
Cut 2

C
YOKE
Cut 2

centre front

1 square = 1 inch   89   *Angel top*

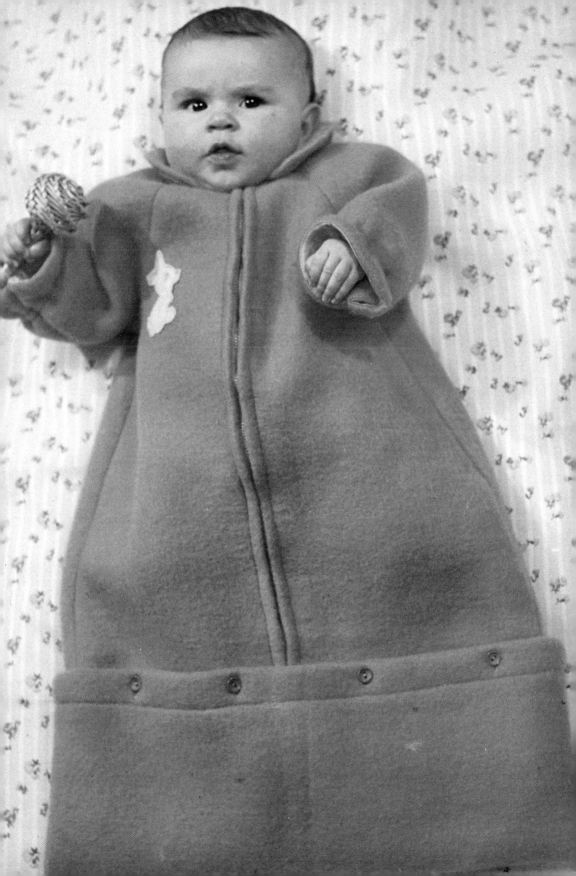

Snug sleeping bag

Made in brushed wool fabric, this cosy bag keeps a baby warm in his perambulator if he is inclined to kick the covers off and is an ideal travelling outfit. This size is for a six month old baby, with an approximate length of 24 inches.

Materials required:

$1\frac{5}{8}$ yards 36-inch wide fabric.
20 inch open end zip fastener.
$8 \times \frac{1}{2}$-inch buttons.
Coats Bias binding.
1 hook and eye.
$\frac{1}{4}$-inch elastic for wrists.
Coats Drima thread.

Cutting directions

Make paper pattern from graph pattern
1 square = 1 inch. $\frac{5}{8}$ inch seam allowance included.
Pattern A – Front cut 2.
Pattern B – Back cut 1.
Pattern C – Collar cut 2.
Pattern D – Sleeve cut 2.
Pattern E – Bag bottom cut 1.

Sleeping bag

To make up

1. Strengthen button positions by basting bias binding to the wrong sides of Front and Back section on button line.
2. Sew binding to wrong sides of sleeve pieces to make wrist casings.
3. Make narrow hems on sleeve edges.
4. Stitch sleeves to Front and Back sections, right sides facing.
5. Place collar section together right sides facing. Stitch the curved edge. Turn to right side. Top stitch $\frac{1}{4}$ inch from curved edge.
6. Join collar section to neck edge.
7. Insert zip fastener at Centre Front and continue machine stitching to lower edge of section.
8. Insert elastic through wrist casings. Stitch ends to sleeve.
9. Stitch entire underarm and side seams in one continuous seam.
10. Make a narrow hem on lower edge.
11. Fold bottom bag section in half, right sides facing. Baste and stitch short ends.
12. Make hems on long edges. Turn to right side.
13. Make 8 buttonholes, 4 on front, 4 on back. Sew buttons to correspond.

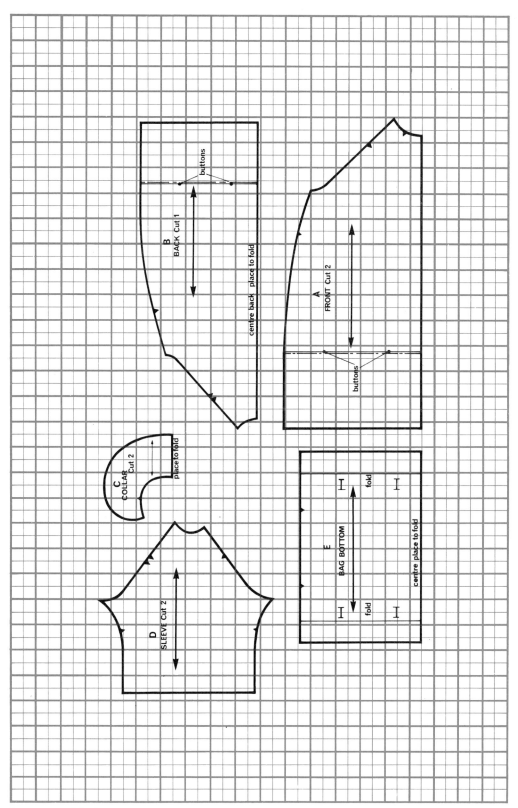

1 square = 1 inch

93

Teenager's suit

A very easy-to-make trouser and waistcoat outfit for girls aged 12 to 15 years.

The size of the graph pattern will fit bust 30 inches, waist 25½ inches and hips 32 inches, with the finished length of the trousers, from the waist, 36 inches. The pattern can be both lengthened and enlarged to fit older girls. The suit shown has been made up in a hard-wearing denim fabric, but you can use almost any fabric from cotton velvet to seersucker and it will still look smart and be comfortable. Made in a plain fabric, the waistcoat lends itself well to all kinds of decoration, from appliqué motifs to embroidery in Raffene.

Materials required:

Trousers:

2¼ yards 36-inch wide fabric.
6-inch zip fastener.
Elastic, ¼ inch wide to fit back waist measurement plus 2 inches.
1 hook and bar fastener.
Coats Drima thread.

Waistcoat:

1¼ yards 36-inch wide fabric.
1¼ yards 36-inch wide lining fabric.
Coats Drima thread.

Cutting directions

Make a paper pattern from graph pattern 1 square = 1 inch. ⅝ inch seam allowance has been included.

Trousers
Pattern A – Front cut 2.
Pattern B – Back cut 2.
Pattern C – Front Facing cut 1

Waistcoat
Pattern D – Front cut 4, (2 from lining).
Pattern E – Back cut 2, (1 from lining).

To make up

Trousers
1. Baste and stitch darts on front sections.
2. Stitch Centre Front seam.
3. Stitch front facing to front waist edge, right sides together, turn to wrong side.
4. Baste and stitch Centre Back seam.
5. Fold back waist edge on fold line to inside. Baste and stitch a ½-inch casing. Insert elastic inside casing. Secure at both ends.
6. Join front section to back at side seams, making sure that front facing is not caught in the seam. Leave left side open for zip.
7. Insert zip fastener.
8. Turn down waist facing, turn in ends and sew to seams.
9. Sew hook and bar above zip fastener. Make hems on trouser ends.

Waistcoat
1. Stitch Front to Back at side seams.
2. Stitch front lining to back lining at side seams, leaving part of the seam unstitched for turning inside out.
3. Press shoulder seam allowance to the wrong side.
4. Place lining on outer fabric sections, right sides facing. Stitch all edges except the shoulder edges. Turn to right side through opening in side seam. Slipstitch seam closed.
5. Stitch shoulder seams of outer fabric section, right sides together. Trim seams. Slip seam allowance under lining. Slipstitch shoulder edges of lining together.

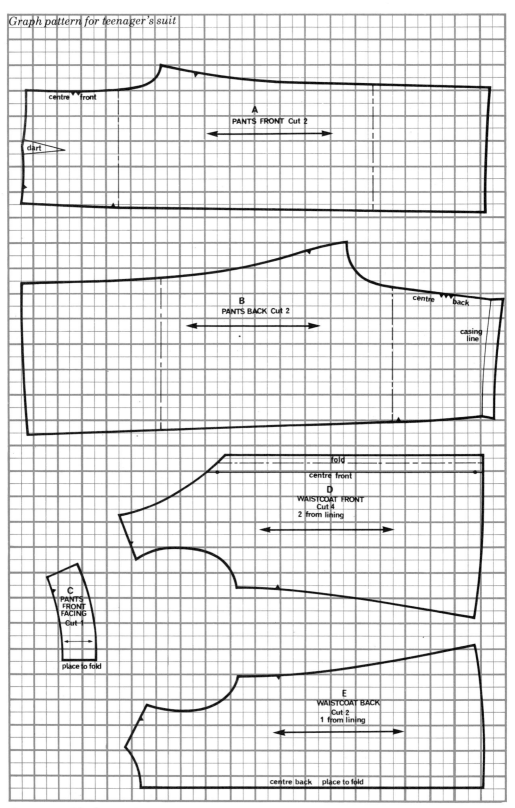

centre front

A
PANTS FRONT Cut 2

dart

B
PANTS BACK Cut 2

centre   back

casing
line

fold

centre front

D
WAISTCOAT FRONT
Cut 4
2 from lining

C
PANTS
FRONT
FACING
Cut 1

place to fold

E
WAISTCOAT BACK
Cut 2
1 from lining

centre back   place to fold

1 square = 1 inch   96

Child's trouser suit

This trouser suit is styled so that it can be worn either by a boy or a girl, depending on the fabric chosen. For a girl, the sleeves can be left out of the bodice and the armholes finished with bias-cut binding, to make a sleeveless summer suit.

Measurements

Chest 23 inches; Waist 21 inches; Top length from neck to hem 16 inches.
Trousers – finished length from waist $24\frac{1}{2}$ inches.

Materials required

Top
$1\frac{1}{8}$ yards 45-inch wide fabric.
$3 \times \frac{1}{2}$-inch buttons.
7-inch zip fastener.

Trousers
$1\frac{5}{8}$ yards 36-inch wide fabric
$\frac{5}{8}$ yard elastic $\frac{3}{4}$-inch wide.
Coats Drima thread.

Cutting directions

Make a paper pattern from the graph pattern 1 square = 1 inch. $\frac{5}{8}$ inch seam allowance included.
Trousers
Pattern A – Front cut 2.
Pattern B – Back cut 2.

Top
Pattern C – Front cut 1
Pattern D – Back cut 2.
Pattern E – Front cut 1.
Pattern F – Back facing cut 2.
Pattern G – Tab cut 1
Pattern H – Sleeve cut 2.

To make up

Top
1. Stitch Centre Back seam leaving opening for zip fastener.
2. Make up tab as follows: turn in seam allowance on two long sides and short straight edge. Press. Baste in place to top front neck edge, matching centres. Stitch in position.
3. Join Back to Front at shoulder seams.
4. Join front facing to back facing at shoulder seams.
5. Stitch facing to neck edge, right sides facing. Turn to inside and catch facing to shoulder seams.
6. Insert zip fastener at centre back seam; avoid catching neck facing.
7. Turn in neck facing short ends, stitch to zip tape.
8. Stitch sleeves in armholes at the sleeve crown.
9. Stitch sleeve seams and side seams in one continuous seam.
10. Hem sleeve edges.
11. Hem lower edge of top.
12. Sew buttons to front tab.

Trousers
1. Join one front section to one back section at side and inner leg seams.
2. Place one leg inside the other, right sides together. Stitch centre seam.
3. Stitch $1\frac{1}{2}$-inch casing at waist, leaving opening for inserting elastic.
4. Insert elastic, overlap ends, stitch securely by hand.
5. Close casing opening. Make hem on leg sections.

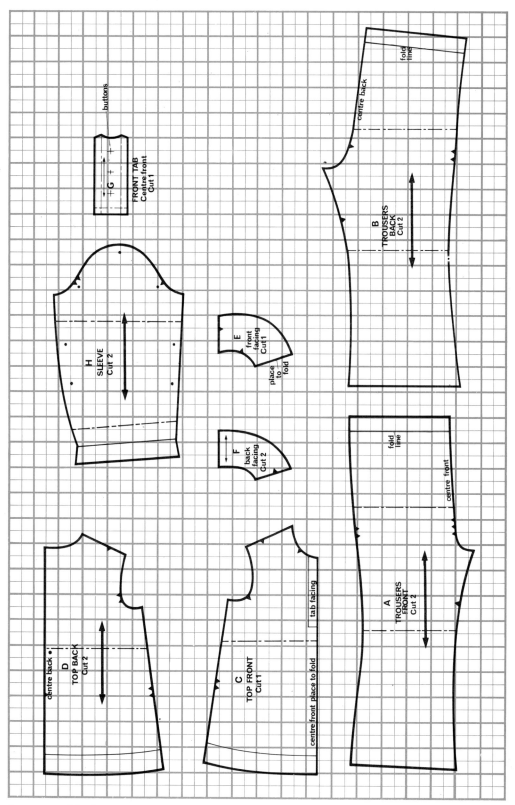

buttons

FRONT TAB
Centre front
Cut 1

G

centre back

fold line

B
TROUSERS
BACK
Cut 2

H
SLEEVE
Cut 2

E
front
facing
Cut 1

place
to
fold

F
back
facing
Cut 2

fold
line

centre front

centre back

D
TOP BACK
Cut 2

C
TOP FRONT
Cut 1

tab facing

centre front place to fold

A
TROUSERS
FRONT
Cut 2

1 square = 1 inch

99

Pleated party dress

This pattern makes up well in cotton or light-weight wool fabrics for day wear but made with a full length skirt and in cotton voile, it is a perfect style for a bridesmaid's dress. The sleeves can be left out of the bodice for a sleeveless summer style.

Measurements

Chest 24 inches; Waist 21½ inches; Hips 25 inches; Finished length 22 inches.

Materials required:

1⅝ yards 36 inch wide fabric.
¼ yard fabric for yoke lining (this can be the same as the top fabric, in which case 2⅛ yards altogether is required).
14 inch zip fastener.
Coats Drima thread.

Cutting directions

Make paper pattern from graph pattern
1 square = 1 inch. ⅝ inch seam allowance included.
Pattern A – Front yoke cut 2 (1 for lining).
Pattern B – Back yoke cut 4 (2 for lining).
Pattern C – Front skirt cut 1.
Pattern D – Back skirt cut 2.
Pattern E – Sleeve cut 2.

French seams should be used, otherwise use plain seams.

To make up

1. Make pleats on Front Skirt section as follows: fold along solid lines and bring to meet the broken lines, working on the right side of the fabric. Press. Baste along top edge.
2. Join Front fabric Yoke section to Front Skirt, matching centres. Press seam upwards.
3. Stitch Centre Back seam of skirt leaving opening for zip fastener.
4. Make pleats on Back Skirt following the same method as for front.
5. Stitch Back Yoke fabric section to Back Skirt matching centres. Press seam upwards.
6. Join Front to Back at shoulder seams.
7. Join front lining yoke to back lining yoke at shoulder seams. Press seam allowance to wrong side at lower edges.
8. Place lining yoke to dress yoke right sides facing. Stitch Centre Back edges and neck edge. Clip curves, trim and turn to wrong side. Sew lining to yoke above machine stitching.
9. Insert zip fastener.
10. Join Front to Back at side seams. Stitch sleeve seams.
11. Make hems on sleeve edges.
13. Insert sleeves in bodice armholes.
14. Make hem on lower edge.

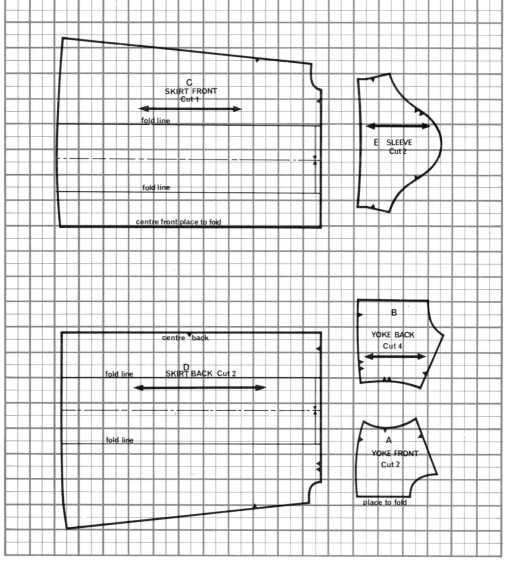

C
SKIRT FRONT
Cut 1

fold line

fold line

centre front place to fold

E SLEEVE
Cut 2

B
YOKE BACK
Cut 4

centre back

D
SKIRT BACK Cut 2

fold line

fold line

A
YOKE FRONT
Cut 2

place to fold

1 square = 1 inch

101

Child's pleated dress

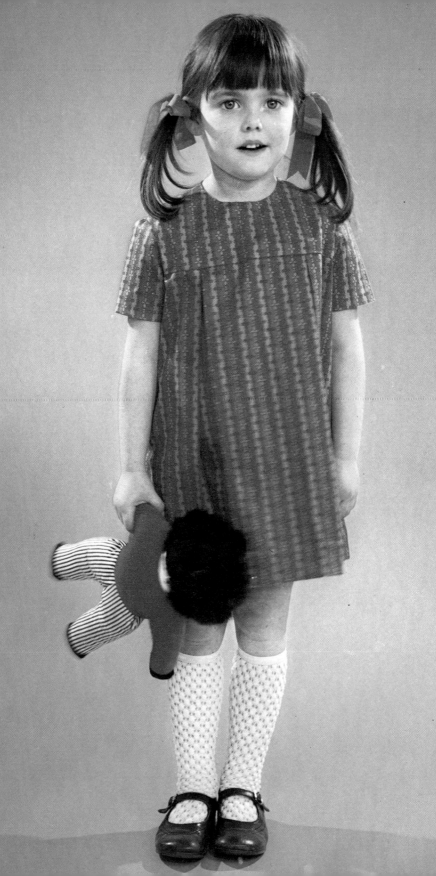

Adaptable child's dress

A very straightforward dress like this can be made up in different colours and take a little girl through school days and holidays alike. The neckline can be finished off with bias-cut binding, with a narrow trimming or, if preferred, with a Peter Pan collar. Make the collar up in piqué and keep it as a detachable trim for a quick way of making the dress look different.

Measurements

Chest 23 inches; Waist 21 inches; Finished back length from neck to hem 20 inches.

Materials required:

1¼ yards 45-inch wide fabric.
12-inch zip fastener.
1⅛ yards trimming for version illustrated.
Coats Drima thread.

Cutting directions

Make paper pattern from graph pattern
1 square = 1 inch. ⅝ inch seam allowance.
included.
Pattern A – Front bodice cut 1.
Pattern B – Back bodice cut 2.
Pattern C – Front neck facing cut 1.
Pattern D   Back neck facing cut 2.
Pattern E – Skirt Front cut 1.
Pattern F – Skirt back cut 2.
Pattern G – Sleeve cut 2.
Pattern H – Peter Pan collar cut 4.

To make up

1. Baste and stitch Back Bodice darts.
2. Stitch shoulder seams and side seams of Front bodice to Back bodice.
3. Stitch Centre Back seam of skirt leaving part of the seam open for inserting the zip.
4. Stitch side seams of Front skirt and Back skirt.
5. Pin bodice to skirt, right sides facing. Stitch side seams to join.
6. Insert zip fastener at Centre Back.
7. Join front neck facing to back neck facing at shoulder seams.
8. Place neck facing to neck edge, right sides together. Stitch, grade seams, clip curves, turn to inside. Catch facing to shoulder seams and to zip fastener tape.
9. Stitch sleeve seams.
10. Hem sleeve edges.
11. Insert sleeves in bodice.
Make skirt hem and stitch on trimming to cover seams if required. Make up Peter Pan collar as instructed on page 44.

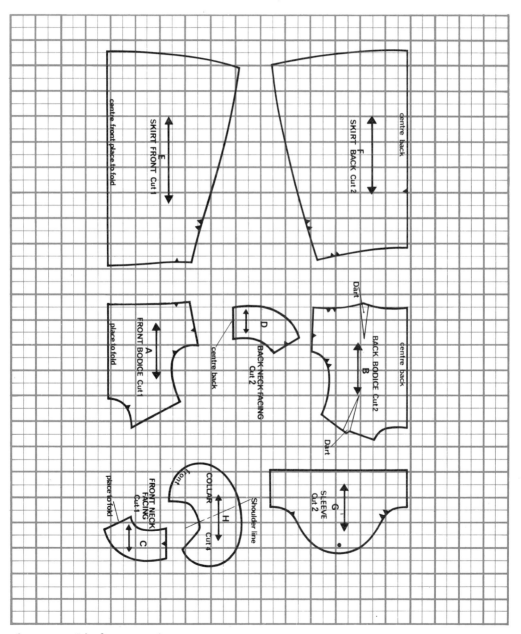

centre back

SKIRT BACK Cut 2

F

SKIRT FRONT Cut 1

E

centre front place to fold

place to fold

FRONT BODICE Cut 1

A

centre back

D

BACK NECK FACING Cut 2

Dart

BACK BODICE Cut 2

B

centre back

Dart

place to fold

FRONT NECK FACING Cut 1

C

front

COLLAR Cut 4

H

Shoulder line

SLEEVE Cut 2

G

1 square = 1 inch

105

Toddler's dungarees

Dungarees, made in a hardwearing cotton needlecord keep a small child trim-looking, warm and comfortable. Make sure that you choose a non-shrink and washable fabric and make the play trousers for either a boy or a girl.

Measurements

Chest 21 inches; Waist 20 inches.

Materials required

$1\frac{1}{8}$ yards 36-inch wide fabric.
$4 \times \frac{1}{2}$-inch buttons.
12 inches $\frac{3}{4}$-inch wide elastic.
Coats Drima thread.

Cutting directions

Make a paper pattern from graph pattern 1 square = 1 inch. $\frac{5}{8}$ inch seam allowance has been included.
Pattern A – Front cut 2.
Pattern B – Back cut 2.
Pattern C – Bib cut 2.
Pattern D – Front waistband cut 1.
Pattern E – Suspender strap cut 2.
Pattern F – Pocket cut 2.

To make up

1. Join Centre Front seam.
2. Neaten pocket facing; turn under $\frac{1}{4}$ inch on upper edge and top stitch. Turn upper edge of pocket to right side along fold line and baste to make facing. Stitch along facing at side edges. Turn facing to wrong side. Press under remaining raw edges to wrong side.
3. Stitch pockets in place on front.
4. Stitch bib sections together, right sides facing, leaving one long edge open to turn. Trim seams and corners. Turn to right side.
5. Baste bib to wrong side of Front.
6. Join Centre Back seam of trousers.
7. Stitch Front to Back at side seams. Clip seam allowance to dot. Press seam open below clips and towards fronts above clip.
8. Stitch inner leg seams.
9. Stitch hem at waist back to form 1-inch casing for elastic.
10. Insert elastic and adjust to fit. Stitch elastic to trousers through all thicknesses of fabric.
11. On Front waistband, press seam allowance to wrong side on long unnotched edge and short ends.
12. Baste wrong side of trousers front to right side of band. Stitch and press seam upwards.
13. Turn band to outside, baste pressed edges over seams. Topstitch all edges of the band.
14. Fold suspender straps in half lengthwise, right sides facing. Baste and stitch taking $\frac{3}{8}$-inch seams and leaving opening for turning. Turn to right side and slipstitch to close.
15. Make a buttonhole at the shaped end of both suspender straps. Sew a button to the square end of both suspender straps.
16. Sew two buttons to inside of back top edge of trousers as marked on pattern.
17. Make buttonholes in bib at each top corner.
18. Make hem on trouser edges.

Graph pattern for toddler's dungarees

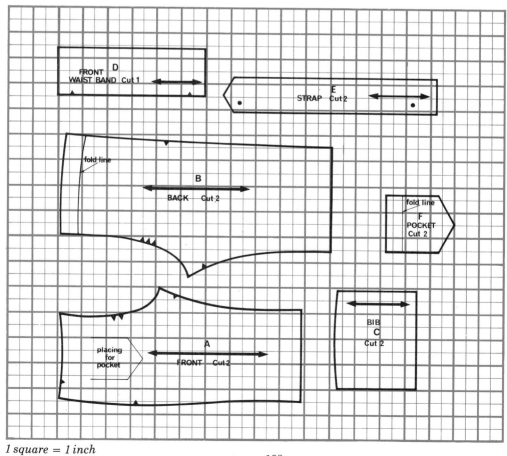

1 square = 1 inch

Pinafore dress

This is a very easy dress to make and is so simply designed that the style can be made up in a variety of fabrics for different occasions. For an alternative way with the pattern, cut the dress short at the hipline to make a useful jerkin to wear over trousers. Leave the last four inches of the side seams unstitched for greater ease of movement and catch-stitch the seam allowances back. Finish the hem off in the usual way.

Materials required:

1⅝ yards 54 inch wide fabric.
18 inch zip fastener.
1 hook and eye.
Coats Drima thread

Cutting directions

Make a paper pattern from the graph pattern, 1 square = 1 inch. ⅝ inch seam allowance has been included.
Pattern A – Front cut 2 pieces
Pattern B – Back cut 1 piece.
Pattern C – Armhole facing cut 2 pieces.
Pattern D – Front neck facing cut 2 pieces.
Pattern E – Back neck facing cut 1 piece.

To make up

1. Stitch darts on front and back sections.
2. Baste and stitch Centre Front seam leaving 18 inches below the spot open for the insertion of the zip fastener.
3. Join dress shoulder seams.
4. Join Back and Front facing on shoulder seams.
5. Baste and stitch facing to neckline and front edges of dress, taking ¼ inch seam on the front edge.
6. Insert zip fastener at Centre Front. Sew hook and eye above zip to secure.
7. Baste and stitch side seams.
8. Stitch short ends of armhole facings.
9. Place facings in corresponding armhole right sides facing. Baste and stitch. Turn facings to the inside of the garment and catch to seams at shoulder and underarm. Finish hem.

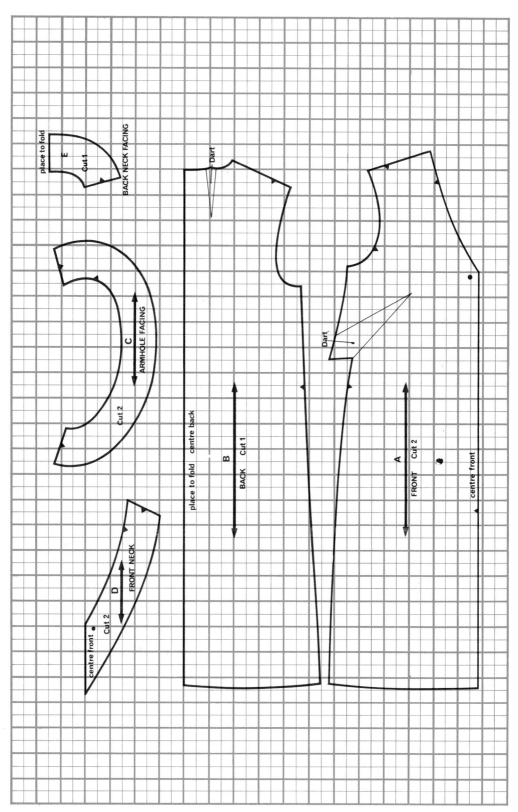

place to fold

E
Cut 1

BACK NECK FACING

ARMHOLE FACING

C

Cut 2

Dart

place to fold   centre back

B

BACK   Cut 1

Dart,

A

FRONT   Cut 2

centre front

FRONT NECK

D

Cut 2

centre front

1 square = 1 inch

110

Shirt-style blouse

Make this classically styled blouse with the convertible collar to wear under the pinafore dress, with a skirt or tucked into trousers. As an adaptation, the waist could be extended to make a full length dress, to be worn with a belt.

Materials required:

3 yards 36 inch wide fabric.
Interfacing for collar and cuffs.
10 $\frac{5}{8}$-inch buttons.
Coats Drima thread.

Cutting directions

Make a paper pattern from the graph pattern
1 square = 1 inch.
$\frac{5}{8}$ inch seam allowances have been included.
Pattern A – Front cut 2.
Pattern B – Back cut 1.
Pattern C – Collar cut 3 (1 from interfacing).
Pattern D – Cuff cut 6 (2 from interfacing).
Pattern E – Sleeve cut 2.

To make up

1. Stitch darts on Back section.
2. Make two rows of gathering stitches between notches on Front shoulder edge.
3. Pull up gathers on Front shoulder sections to fit Back shoulder sections. Stitch Back to Front at shoulders.
4. Join Front to Back at side seams.
5. Fold Front facing Back to wrong side. Baste.
6. Make up interfaced collar and stitch to neckline.
7. Stitch fabric facing to sleeve edges on right side of fabric extending over dots. Clip into edge to dots and turn facing to the wrong side.
8. Stitch sleeve seams.
9. Gather sleeve heads.
10. Make up cuffs and attach to sleeves. Make buttonholes on cuffs and sew on buttons to correspond.
11. Insert sleeves in blouse armholes.
12. Hem lower edge of blouse.
13. Top-stitch collar and cuff edges if desired.
14. Make 6 buttonholes on right Front of blouse and stitch buttons to correspond.

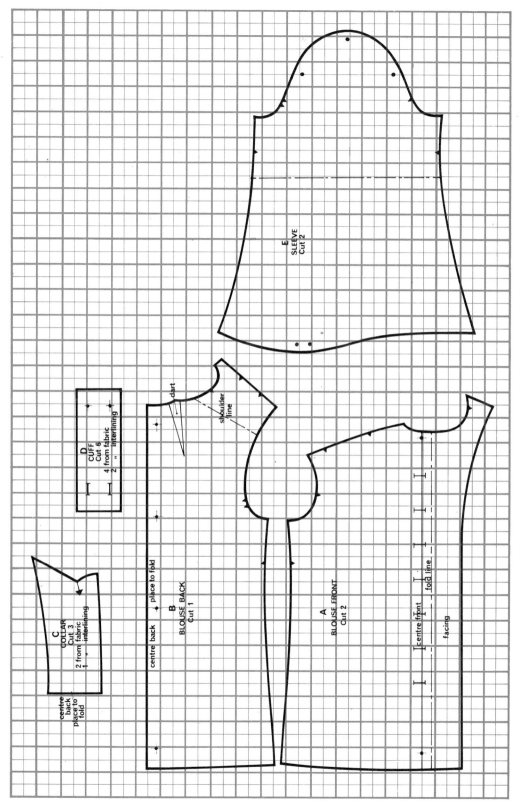

E
SLEEVE
Cut 2

D
CUFF
Cut 6
4 from fabric
2 " interlining

dart

shoulder
line

place to fold

centre back

B
BLOUSE BACK
Cut 1

C
COLLAR
Cut 3
2 from fabric
1 " interlining

centre
back
place to
fold

A
BLOUSE FRONT
Cut 2

centre front

fold line

facing

1 square = 1 inch

Shirt-style blouse

Classic suit

This is a suit line which is a perennial favourite and never seems to go out of fashion. It is an easy style to sew and you'll enjoy every moment of making it. The suit illustrated was made in a non-crushable woven Terylene fabric with a linen finish but most woven fabrics will do for this style. If a very loosely woven fabric is chosen, then the jacket will have to be lined.

For a distinctive look, trim the edges of the jacket with a chunky looking braid.

Materials required:

2½ yards of 54-inch wide fabric.
Interfacing for front and back neck facings.
8-inch zip fastener.
2 hooks and eyes.
1-inch Petersham ribbon, to waist measurement plus turnings.
Coats Drima thread.

Cutting directions

Make paper pattern from graph pattern
1 square = 1 inch.
$\frac{5}{8}$ inch seam allowances included.
Pattern A – Jacket front cut 2.
Pattern B – Jacket back cut 1.
Pattern C – Upper sleeve section cut 2.
Pattern D – Under sleeve section cut 2.
Pattern E – Front facing cut 4 (2 from interfacing).
Pattern F – Back neck facing cut 2 (1 from interfacing).
Pattern G – Lower pocket cut 2.
Pattern H – Upper pocket cut 2.
Pattern J – Front skirt cut 1.
Pattern K – Back skirt cut 2.

To make up

Jacket
1. Stitch darts on Front and Back sections.
2. Stitch Centre Back seam.
3. Make pockets up and stitch to jacket fronts.
4. Baste Front facing interfacing to wrong side of Front section. Baste interfacing for Back neck section to wrong side of Back neck.
5. Join shoulder seams to Back and Front.
6. Stitch shoulder seams of fabric Front facing to fabric Back neck facing.
7. Place facing to jacket, right sides together. Baste and stitch front and neck edges. Clip seams, grade and turn to right side.
8. Join side seams of Front and Back sections.
9. Stitch Upper sleeve to Lower sleeve sections.
10. Hem sleeve edges.
11. Insert sleeves in jacket armholes.
12. Hem lower edge of jacket.
13. Neaten all inside seams.

Skirt
1. Stitch darts on Front and Back sections.
2. Stitch Centre Back seam.
3. Join Front to Back at side seams, leaving left side open at top for zip.
4. Insert zip fastener.
5. Make ½ inch hems on the ends of petersham and insert petersham band in skirt waist.
6. Sew hooks and eyes at waist fastening.
7. Make hem.
8. Neaten all seams.

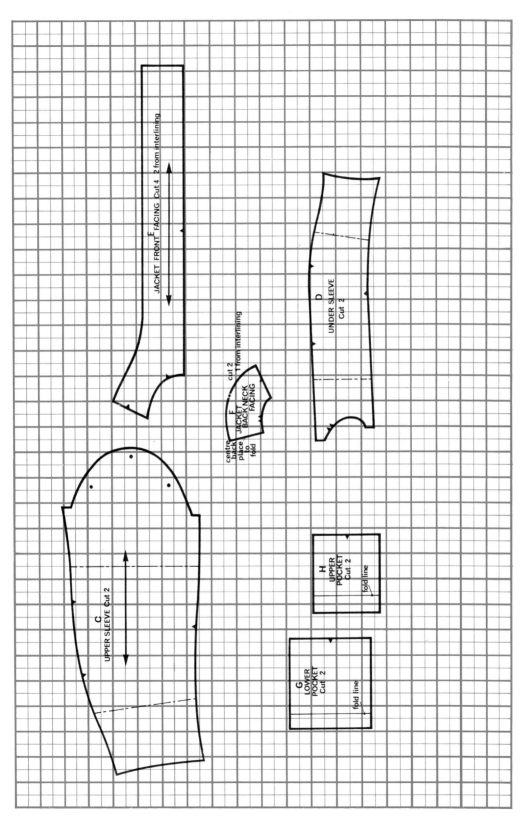

JACKET FRONT FACING Cut 4 2 from interlining

E

F cut 2 1 from interlining

JACKET
BACK NECK
FACING

centre
back
place
to
fold

D

UNDER SLEEVE
Cut 2

C

UPPER SLEEVE Cut 2

H

UPPER
POCKET
Cut 2

fold line

G

LOWER
POCKET
Cut 2

fold line

1 square = 1 inch

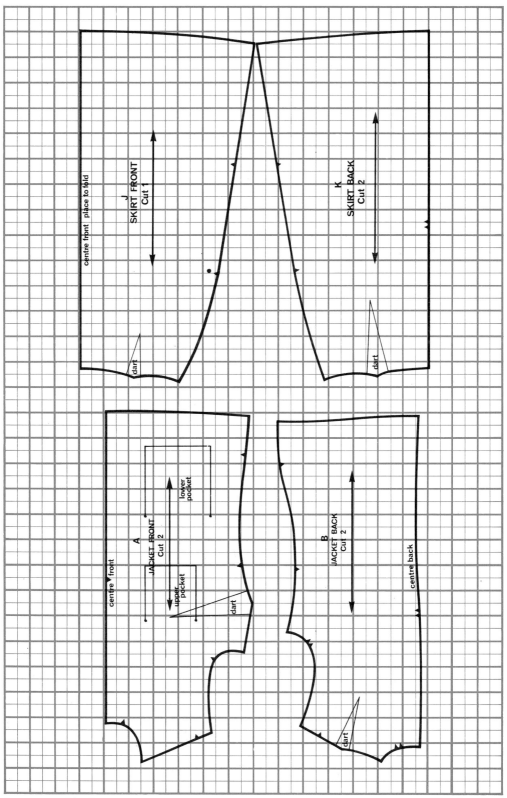

centre front place to fold

J
SKIRT FRONT
Cut 1

K
SKIRT BACK
Cut 2

dart

dart

centre ▼ front

A
JACKET FRONT
Cut 2

lower pocket

upper pocket

dart

B
JACKET BACK
Cut 2

centre back

dart

1 square = 1 inch

117

Classic suit

Trouser suit

A perfect suit for sports wear, for holidays and for any occasion where you want to look smart and feel comfortable.

Materials required:

Trousers
1½ yards 54-inch wide fabric.
9-inch zip fastener.
Interfacing for waist edge.
1 hook and eye.
Coats Drima thread.

Jacket
2 yards 54-inch wide fabric.
Lining for pocket.
6 × 1-inch buttons.
Interfacing for Front and neck edges.
1 snap fastener.
Coats Drima thread.

Cutting directions

Make paper pattern from the graph pattern
1 square = 1 inch.
⅝-inch seam allowance included.

Trousers
Pattern A – Front cut 2.
Pattern B – Back cut 2.
Pattern C – Front waist facing cut 2 (1 from interfacing).
Pattern D – Back waist facing cut 2 (1 from interfacing).

Jacket
Pattern E – Front cut 2.
Pattern F – Back cut 2.
Pattern G – Sleeves cut 2.
Pattern H – Back neck facing cut 4 (2 from interfacing) .
Pattern J – Pocket cut 4 (2 from interfacing).

To make up

Trousers
1. Stitch darts on Front and Back sections.

2. Stitch one Front section to one Back section at side and Inner leg seams. Repeat with other sections but leaving Left side open at top for zip.
3. Place one leg inside the other, Right sides facing. Stitch Centre seam.
4. Stitch Front interfacing to Back interfacing at short ends to form waist facing. Leave Left side open. Repeat with facing sections.
5. Baste interfacing to waist edge on wrong side of fabric.
6. Stitch facing to waist edge, right sides together. Trim, clip grade and turn to wrong side.
7. Insert zip fastener.
Make hems on trouser edges.

Jacket
Baste Front interfacings to wrong sides of Front sections along fold line. Sew lightly in position along fold line.
2. Slash along dart line as shown on pattern.
3. Stitch darts on Back and Front sections.
4. Baste Back interfacings to wrong sides of Back neck edges.
5. Stitch Centre back seam .
6. Join shoulder seams of Front and Back.
7. Stitch Centre back seams of facing.
8. Stitch Back facing to Front facing at shoulders.
9. Fold Front facing to outside of jacket, right sides together. Baste and stitch neck edge. Turn to wrong side.
10. Make hem on lower edge.
11. Stitch sleeve seams.
12. Insert sleeves in armholes.
13. Hem sleeve edges.
14. Make up pockets and stitch to jacket.
15. Make buttonholes to right side of jacket and sew buttons on left side to correspond.
16. Attach snap fastener at top edge of jacket neck to secure.

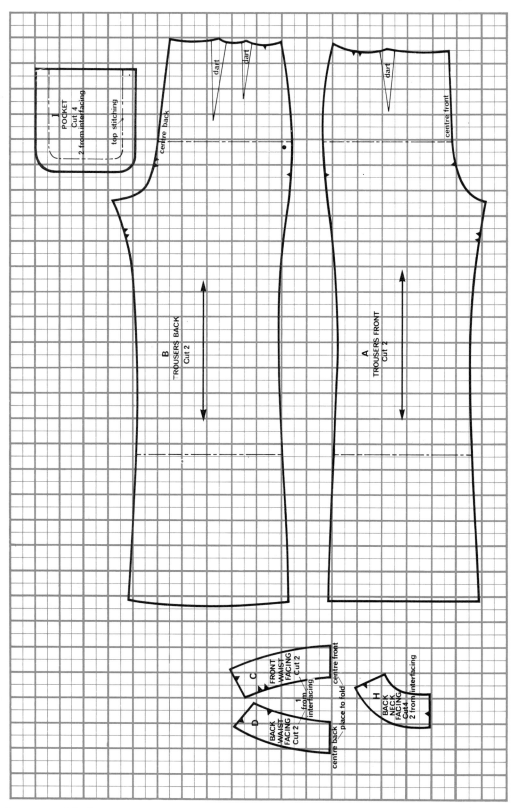

POCKET
Cut 4
2 from interfacing
top stitching
I

dart

dart

dart

centre back

centre front

B
TROUSERS BACK
Cut 2

A
TROUSERS FRONT
Cut 2

C
FRONT
WAIST
FACING
Cut 2

1
from
interfacing

centre front

D
BACK
WAIST
FACING
Cut 2

centre back

place to fold

H
BACK
NECK
FACING
Cut 4
2 from interfacing

1 square = 1 inch

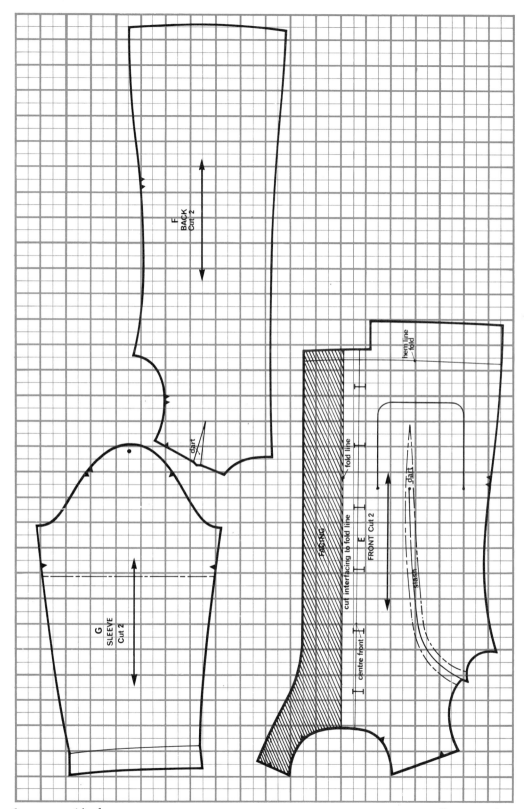

F
BACK
Cut 2

dart

G
SLEEVE
Cut 2

FACING

cut interfacing to fold line

fold line

hem line
fold

E
FRONT Cut 2

dart

slash

centre front

1 square = 1 inch

Trouser suit

Pleated skirt

Pleats are interesting to do and not as difficult as they look at first sight. The secret of success is in the pinning, pressing and basting.

Materials required

$1\frac{1}{4}$ yards 54 inch wide fabric.
Interfacing for waistband.
8-inch zip fastener.

2 hooks and eyes
Coats Drima thread.

Cutting directions

Make paper pattern from graph pattern
1 square = 1 inch.
$\frac{5}{8}$ inch seam allowance has been included.
Pattern A – Front cut 1.
Pattern B – Back cut 1.
Pattern C – Side Front cut 2.
Pattern D – Side Back cut 2.
Pattern E – Waistband cut 1 plus piece from interfacing the length of the waistband by $1\frac{1}{2}$ inches deep.

Pleated skirt

To make up

1. Stitch darts on Side Front sections.
2. Place Side Fronts to Front sections. Baste and stitch Side Front seams.
To make pleat nearest Side Front seam, baste and stitch Side Fronts to Front to X, matching pleat line. Press towards Centre.
3. To make pleats nearest the Centre Front; baste and stitch pleats lines together to X. Press towards Centre.
4. Baste upper edges through all thicknesses.
5. Make up Back sections in the same way stitching Side Back panels to the Back panel and pleating as above.
6. Stitch Front to Back at side seams leaving side open for zip fastener.
7. Insert zip fastener.
8. Place interfacing to the wrong side of waistband with one long edge of interfacing to one long edge of waistband. Sew interfacing to fabric at long inner edge. Press seam upwards.
9. Fold waistband in half right sides together. Baste and stitch the short ends and along Back for 2 inches. Turn to right side.
10. Attach waistband to skirt at waist edge.
11. Stitch hooks and eyes at waist opening.
12. Pin up hem. Clip Side Front and Side Back seams to top edge of hem. Press seams open below the clips. Make hem.

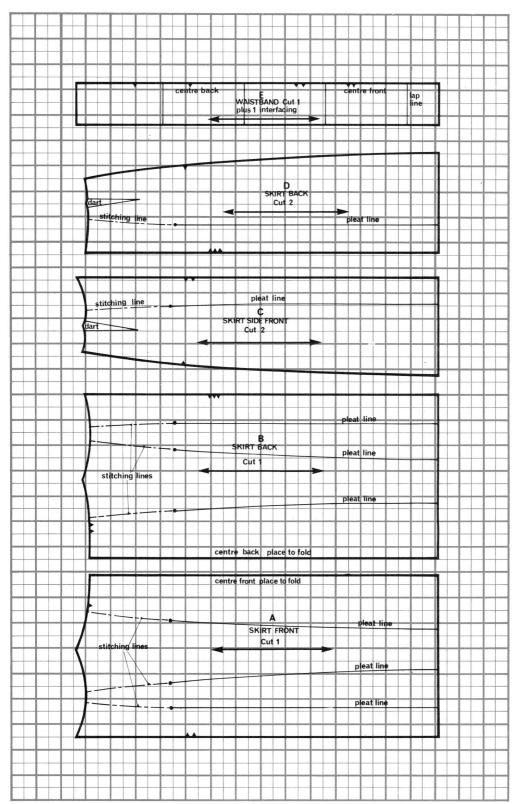

centre back

E
WAISTBAND Cut 1
plus 1 interfacing

centre front

lap
line

D
SKIRT BACK
Cut 2

dart

stitching line

pleat line

stitching line

pleat line

C
SKIRT SIDE FRONT
Cut 2

dart

B
SKIRT BACK

pleat line

pleat line

Cut 1

stitching lines

pleat line

centre back   place to fold

centre front place to fold

A
SKIRT FRONT
Cut 1

pleat line

stitching lines

pleat line

pleat line

1 square = 1 inch

125

Index